CONTENTS

INTRODUCTION

My entire life can be summed up in three words: Weight loss diets. I tried every diet known to men – from keto and paleo diet to the cabbage soup diet. Seriously, I did it all. But the results were, to put it mildly, devastating. I want to lose weight no matter what it took because I was desperate. Over the years, I have found a few strategies that seem to be effective. However, they were short-lived and I have experienced weight cycling, also known as "yo-yo dieting". However, I did not know anything about food and nutrition. I did not know anything about my body and weight loss process. I didn't know that restrictive diets lead to increased appetite as the body loses muscle mass, trying to resupply depleted fat stores. Moreover, yo-yo dieting has harmful effects on our health; it has been associated with increased risk of heart diseases, diabetes, and fatty liver; in fact, weight fluctuations may be worse than staying overweight. With this in mind, I decided to break the cycle of weight fluctuations with temporary success, and start thinking in terms of long-term lifestyle changes. First things first, I decide to change the way I cook my favorite food. I like home-cooked meals but I don't want to be occupied in the kitchen for hours. On the other hand, I like popular fast-food items such as burgers, French fries, pizza, and donuts. I wanted to drop my pounds but not miss out on my guilty pleasure foods. Therefore, an Air Fryer seemed to be working. I must confess, I was skeptical at first, but this small countertop convection oven seemed like a perfect solution to my problems with obesity and a great way to avoid consuming excessive calories. Besides being economical and practical, I found an Air Fryer perfect tool for family gatherings and children's birthday parties. Today, I can't imagine healthy dieting without an Air Fryer. It delivers a crispy finished product and flavor-packed meals without all that unhealthy oil. Isn't it fantastic?

In this cookbook, I have a tendency to promote a healthy lifestyle and traditional values, without starving and nutrient depletion. Family dinners bring families together, contributing to our physical and mental health. Did you know that a child who is engaged in the cooking process with parents is more likely to grow to be an adult who has healthy eating habits? This is the recipe collection I wish I had when I started my weight loss journey. It is all about my favorite Air Fryer recipes, including my personal experience with this unique kitchen tool. I started by making fried vegetables and chicken wings in it. Then I ventured into more complicated meals such as casserole and pastry. For this recipe collection, I chose easy-to-follow recipes with fewer ingredients so a family dinner can be a reality any night of the week. Are you searching for a way to simplify your cooking routine? Do you want recipes for the best "make-it-again" fried food? Well, you are in the right place. The Air Fryer and this recipe collection are ready to be your reliable kitchen companions! The Air Fryer will spark your imagination and create heart-warming family kitchen memories! Enjoy!

Getting to Know Your Air Fryer and 5 Must-Know Tips

I'm asked two questions time and time again, "Why use an Air Fryer? Is an Air Fryer worth buying?" Well, I have three words for you: Health, convenience, and versatility. Everyone likes the taste of fried foods. Nothing says Saturday movie night better than a big bowl of chips! An air fryer is a modern kitchen appliance, a type of a mini convection oven, used for making fried foods. It offers a flavorful, crispy finished product by circulating hot air in the cooking chamber. In other words, a super-heated air circulates around your food for faster and even cooking results. An Air Fryer promises to take a place of a convection oven, deep fryer, grill, and microwave; this magical appliance also lets you sauté and roast your foods. The best of all – your food does not taste like fat. The Air Fryer uses rapid air technology to cook foods to perfection (crispy exteriors and well-cooked, moist interiors) with a drizzle of healthy oil.

Here are a few tips and hacks you might benefit from:

➤ Needless to say, read the user's manual to make the most of your Air Fryer, even if you are an experienced cook; moreover, it is recommended to consult the manual every now and then, since there are dozens of different models of Air Fryer on the market.

➤ If you are not in a hurry, preheat your Air Fryer to ensure even cooking. Turn it to the desired temperature and allow it to run for around 3 minutes before adding ingredients to the cooking basket.

➤ Do not forget to grease the cooking basket; just brush the cooking basket lightly with a healthy oil; most Air Fryer recipes call for 1/2 teaspoon or less per serving.

➤ Don't overcrowd the basket to promote even cooking; simply cook in batches and shake the basket periodically; you can spritz your food with a nonstick spray halfway through cooking time. One more thing – avoid cooking light items in the Air Fryer since it has a powerful fan on top of the unit, aggressively pushing hot air around your food, through the whole cooking basket. It includes leafy things like spinach and fresh herbs, seasonings, top slices of bread on sandwiches.

➤ You can use your Air Fryer for healthy baked goods such as breakfast pastries and desserts. A 6-in round baking pan and bundt pan are worth investing in; bear in mind that baking pans should fit right inside the cooking basket.

Top Benefits of an Air Fryer You Need to Know

Fast and easy meals.

My Air Fryer helps me to avoid "there's-nothing-to-eat" situation on weeknights. Besides being a next-generation kitchen device, the Air Fryer frees up my time. It has automatic functions, so you don't need to stir food and watch the whole cooking process. Most of the recipes call for shaking the basket or flipping the ingredients halfway through the cooking time. That's it! When the cooking process ends, your Air Fryer will automatically turn off. The Air Fryer can deliver amazing results with minimal hands-on time.

Healthy fast food (improve your health and lose weight).

Really?! Is there such a thing as a healthy fast food? The truth is that it's practically impossible to follow a well-balanced diet when you're eating regularly junk food. On the other hand, cooking at home is associated with healthy eating habits. Your dietary patterns are extremely important on your weight loss journey. The good news is that you can cook French fries, donuts, fish, and burgers in your Air Fryer. This is only the beginning. Hearty casseroles, delicious appetizers, and delectable desserts will turn out great in your Air Fryer. When it comes to healthy weight loss that does not compromise flavor, this revolutionary kitchen gadget is a real winner! A lower intake of unhealthy oil is one of the greatest benefits of the Air Fryer. Fried food tastes good, right?! But trans fats are harmful to our health. Fried foods such as chicken nuggets, refrigerated dough, and rolls are high in trans fats. There are numerous negative health effects of eating deep-fried foods such as cardiovascular and coronary diseases, diabetes, obesity, gut microbes, and so on. According to the leading experts, when it comes to healthy dieting, you should not be afraid of fats. You should avoid partially hydrogenated and genetically modified oils such as cottonseed oil, corn oil, and margarine. Good fats include olive oil, avocado oil, nuts and seeds. There are numerous benefits of cooking at home. You can control your portion and count calories more precisely; you can cook with natural and local ingredients. As you probably already know, most pre-packaged foods are high in salt, sodium, sugar and artificial ingredients. Did you know that the spills of used oils injure wildlife, which has harmful effects on our environment? Therefore, our food choices have a direct impact on our health and well-being.

A practical solution to every cooking challenge.

One of the greatest things I love about my Air Fryer is the fact that it cooks food in the sealed environment; it means you can forget about unpleasant kitchen smells! The Air Fryer is good at performing multiple tasks in the kitchen – frying, roasting, grilling, and baking. Some extra-large models can be used for a rotisserie and dehydrating. Plus, unlike the heat in your oven, the heat in the Air Fryer cooking basket is constant; it promotes better and even cooking.

It saves you time and money.

In today's fast-paced world, it seems difficult to follow a healthy diet. I know it. The Air Fryer is a massive time saver. Its easy press-and-go functions save a lot of time in the kitchen. If you're a practical person who doesn't want to spend a fortune on takeaways, you should invest in an Air Fryer. There are many money-saving kitchen tips out there; opt for freezer-friendly recipes that call for local and seasonal ingredients. You can look for items on sale or buy them in bulk. If you have leftover grains or beans, you can make delicious vegan burgers and freeze them in storage containers. This is far less expensive than eating out. The Air Fryer is an energy-efficient kitchen appliance too. To sum up, this is a space, cost, and frustration-saving cooking solution!

Do not give up eating fried foods, your Air Fryer is the perfect alternative to your favorite take-outs and restaurant. If you are thinking of cutting down on fat consumption, the Air Fryer is your number one choice! This is arguably the best way to cook fast food at your own kitchen and eat healthier.

POULTRY RECIPES

Air Fried Chicken With Honey & Lemon

Servings: 6
Cooking Time: 40 Minutes
Ingredients:
- 1 whole chicken, 3 lb
- 2 red and peeled onions
- 2 tbsp olive oil
- 2 apricots
- 1 zucchini
- 1 apple
- 2 cloves finely chopped garlic
- Fresh chopped thyme
- Salt and pepper
- Marinade:
- 5 oz honey
- juice from 1 lemon
- 2 tbsp olive oil
- Salt and pepper

Directions:
1. For the stuffing, chop all ingredients into tiny pieces. Transfer to a large bowl and add the olive oil. Season with salt and pepper. Fill the cavity of the chicken with the stuffing, without packing it tightly.
2. Place the chicken in the air fryer and cook for 10 minutes at 340 F. Warm the honey and the lemon juice in a large pan; season with salt and pepper. Reduce the temperature of the air fryer to 320 F.
3. Brush the chicken with some of the honey-lemon marinade and return it to the fryer. Cook for another 15 minutes; brush the chicken every 5 minutes with the marinade. Serve.

Cauliflower Stuffed Chicken

Servings: 5
Cooking Time: 25 Minutes
Ingredients:
- 1 ½-pound chicken breast, skinless, boneless
- ½ cup cauliflower, shredded
- 1 jalapeno pepper, chopped
- 1 teaspoon ground nutmeg
- 1 teaspoon salt
- ¼ cup Cheddar cheese, shredded
- ½ teaspoon cayenne pepper
- 1 tablespoon cream cheese
- 1 tablespoon sesame oil
- ½ teaspoon dried thyme

Directions:
1. Make the horizontal cut in the chicken breast. In the mixing bowl mix up shredded cauliflower, chopped jalapeno pepper, ground nutmeg, salt, and cayenne pepper. Fill the chicken cut with the shredded cauliflower and secure the cut with toothpicks. Then rub the chicken breast with cream cheese, dried thyme, and sesame oil. Preheat the air fryer to 380F. Put the chicken breast in the air fryer and cook it for 20 minutes. Then sprinkle it with Cheddar cheese and cook for 5 minutes more.

Duck Breast With Figs

Servings: 2
Cooking Time: 45 Minutes
Ingredients:
- 1 pound boneless duck breast
- 6 fresh figs, halved
- 1 tablespoon fresh thyme, chopped
- 2 cups fresh pomegranate juice
- 2 tablespoons lemon juice
- 3 tablespoons brown sugar
- 1 teaspoon olive oil
- Salt and black pepper, as required

Directions:
1. Preheat the Air fryer to 400F and grease an Air fryer basket.
2. Put the pomegranate juice, lemon juice, and brown sugar in a medium saucepan over medium heat.
3. Bring to a boil and simmer on low heat for about 25 minutes.

4. Season the duck breasts generously with salt and black pepper.

5. Arrange the duck breasts into the Air fryer basket, skin side up and cook for about 14 minutes, flipping once in between.

6. Dish out the duck breasts onto a cutting board for about 10 minutes.

7. Meanwhile, put the figs, olive oil, salt, and black pepper in a bowl until well mixed.

8. Set the Air fryer to 400F and arrange the figs into the Air fryer basket.

9. Cook for about 5 more minutes and dish out in a platter.

10. Put the duck breast with the roasted figs and drizzle with warm pomegranate juice mixture.

11. Garnish with fresh thyme and serve warm.

Chestnuts 'n Mushroom Chicken Casserole

Servings: 2
Cooking Time: 35 Minutes
Ingredients:
- 1 (10.75 ounce) can condensed cream of chicken soup
- 1 (4.5 ounce) can mushrooms, drained
- 1 1/2 teaspoons melted butter
- 1 cup shredded, cooked chicken meat
- 1/2 (8 ounce) can water chestnuts, drained (optional)
- 1/2 cup mayonnaise
- 1/2 teaspoon lemon juice
- 1/4 cup shredded Cheddar cheese
- 1/8 teaspoon curry powder
- 1-1/4 cups cooked chopped broccoli

Directions:
1. Lightly grease baking pan of air fryer with cooking spray.

2. Evenly spread broccoli on bottom of pan. Sprinkle chicken on top, followed by water chestnuts and mushrooms.

3. In a bowl, whisk well melted butter, curry powder, lemon juice, mayonnaise, and soup. Pour over chicken mixture in pan. Cover pan with foil.

4. For 25 minutes, cook on 360F.

5. Remove foil from pan and cook for another 10 minutes or until top is a golden brown.

6. Serve and enjoy.

Fried Turkey With Lemon And Herbs

Servings: 6
Cooking Time: 45 Minutes
Ingredients:
- 1 ½ tablespoons yellow mustard
- 1 ½ tablespoons herb seasoning blend
- 1/3 cup tamari sauce
- 1 ½ tablespoons olive oil
- 1/2 lemon, juiced
- 3 turkey drumsticks
- 1/3 cup pear or apple cider vinegar
- 2 sprigs rosemary, chopped

Directions:
1. Dump all ingredients into a mixing dish. Let it marinate overnight.

2. Set your air fryer to cook at 355 degrees F.

3. Season turkey drumsticks with salt and black pepper and roast them at 355 degrees F for 28 minutes. Cook one drumstick at a time.

4. Pause the machine after 14 minutes and flip turkey drumstick. Bon appétit!

Chicken Coconut Meatballs

Servings: 4
Cooking Time: 10 Minutes
Ingredients:
- 1 lb ground chicken
- 1 ½ tsp sriracha
- 1/2 tbsp soy sauce
- 1/2 tbsp hoisin sauce
- ¼ cup shredded coconut
- 1 tsp sesame oil
- ½ cup fresh cilantro, chopped
- 2 green onions, chopped
- Pepper

- Salt

Directions:

1. Spray air fryer basket with cooking spray.
2. Add all ingredients into the large bowl and mix until well combined.
3. Make small balls from meat mixture and place into the air fryer basket.
4. Cook at 350 F for 10 minutes. Turn halfway through.
5. Serve and enjoy.

Chicken With Veggies & Rice

Servings: 3
Cooking Time: 20 Minutes
Ingredients:

- 3 cups cold boiled white rice
- 6 tablespoons soy sauce
- 1 tablespoon vegetable oil
- 1 cup cooked chicken, diced
- ½ cup frozen carrots
- ½ cup frozen peas
- ½ cup onion, chopped

Directions:

1. In a large bowl, add the rice, soy sauce, and oil and mix thoroughly.
2. Add the remaining ingredients and mix until well combined.
3. Transfer the rice mixture into a 7" nonstick pan.
4. Arrange the pan into an Air Fryer basket.
5. Set the temperature of Air Fryer to 360 degrees F.
6. Air Fry for about 20 minutes.
7. Remove the pan from Air Fryer and transfer the rice mixture onto serving plates.
8. Serve immediately.

Copycat Kfc Chicken Strips

Servings: 8
Cooking Time: 20 Minutes
Ingredients:

- 1 chicken breast, cut into strips

- 1 egg, beaten
- 2 tablespoons almond flour
- 2 tablespoons desiccated coconut
- A dash of oregano
- A dash of paprika
- A dash of thyme
- Salt and pepper to taste

Directions:

1. Soak the chicken in egg.
2. In a mixing bowl, combine the rest of the ingredients until well-combined.
3. Dredge the chicken in the dry ingredients.
4. Place in the air fryer basket.
5. Cook for 20 minutes at 350F.

Juicy Turkey Breast Tenderloin

Servings: 3
Cooking Time: 25 Minutes
Ingredients:

- 1 turkey breast tenderloin
- 1/2 tsp sage
- 1/2 tsp smoked paprika
- 1/2 tsp pepper
- 1/2 tsp thyme
- 1/2 tsp salt

Directions:

1. Preheat the air fryer to 350 F.
2. Spray air fryer basket with cooking spray.
3. Rub turkey breast tenderloin with paprika, pepper, thyme, sage, and salt and place in the air fryer basket.
4. Cook for 25 minutes. Turn halfway through.
5. Slice and serve.

Chicken Nuggets

Servings: 4
Cooking Time: 30 Minutes
Ingredients:

- ½ lb. chicken breast, cut into pieces
- 1 tsp. parsley

- 1 tsp. paprika
- 1 tbsp. olive oil
- 2 eggs, beaten
- 1 tsp. tomato ketchup
- 1 tsp. garlic, minced
- ½ cup friendly bread crumbs
- Pepper and salt to taste

Directions:

1. In a bowl, combine the bread crumbs, olive oil, paprika, pepper, and salt.
2. Place the chicken, ketchup, one egg, garlic, and parsley in a food processor and pulse together.
3. Put the other egg in a bowl.
4. Shape equal amounts of the pureed chicken into nuggets. Dredge each one in the egg before coating it in bread crumbs.
5. Put the coated chicken nuggets in the Air Fryer basket and cook at 390°F for 10 minutes.
6. Serve the nuggets hot.

Turkey And Lime Gravy

Servings: 4

Cooking Time: 25 Minutes

Ingredients:

- 1 big turkey breast, skinless, boneless, cubed and browned
- Juice of 1 lime
- Zest of 1 lime, grated
- 1 cup chicken stock
- 3 tablespoons parsley, chopped
- 4 tablespoons butter, melted
- 2 tablespoons thyme, chopped
- A pinch of salt and black pepper

Directions:

1. Heat up a pan that fits the air fryer with the butter over medium heat, add all the ingredients except the turkey, whisk, bring to a simmer and cook for 5 minutes. Add the turkey cubes, put the pan in the air fryer and cook at 380 degrees F for 20 minutes. Divide the meat between plates, drizzle the gravy all over and serve.

Country-fried Chicken Drumsticks

Servings: 4

Cooking Time: 20 Minutes

Ingredients:

- 1 tsp garlic powder
- 1 tsp cayenne pepper
- ½ cup flour
- ¼ cup milk
- ¼ tbsp lemon juice
- Salt and black pepper to taste

Directions:

1. Preheat your Air Fryer to 390 F. Spray the air fryer basket with cooking spray.
2. In a small bowl, mix garlic powder, cayenne pepper, salt, and black pepper. Rub the chicken drumsticks with the mixture. In a separate bowl, combine milk with lemon juice. Pour the flour on a plate.
3. Dunk the chicken in the milk mixture, then roll in the flour to coat
4. Place the chicken in the cooking basket and spray it with cooking spray. Cook for 6 minutes, Slide out the fryer basket and flip; cook for 6 more minutes. Serve cooled.

Pepper Turkey Bacon

Servings: 2

Cooking Time: 8 Minutes

Ingredients:

- 7 oz turkey bacon
- 1 teaspoon coconut oil, melted
- ½ teaspoon ground black pepper

Directions:

1. Slice the turkey bacon if needed and sprinkle it with ground black pepper and coconut oil. Preheat the air fryer to 400F. Arrange the turkey bacon in the air fryer in one layer and cook it for 4 minutes. Then flip the bacon on another side and cook for 4 minutes more.

Authentic Mongolian Chicken

Servings: 5
Cooking Time: 15 Minutes
Ingredients:
- 8 oz flour
- 8 oz breadcrumbs
- 3 beaten eggs
- 4 tbsp canola oil
- Salt and pepper to taste
- 2 tbsp sesame seeds
- 2 tbsp red pepper paste
- 1 tbsp apple cider vinegar
- 2 tbsp honey
- 1 tbsp soy sauce
- Sesame seeds, to serve

Directions:
1. Separate the chicken wings into winglets and drummettes. In a bowl, mix salt, oil and pepper. Preheat your air fryer to a temperature of 350 F. Coat the chicken with beaten eggs followed by breadcrumbs and flour. Place the chicken in air fryer's cooking basket. Spray with a bit of oil and cook for 15 minutes.
2. Mix red pepper paste, apple cider vinegar, soy sauce, honey and ¼ cup of water in a saucepan and bring to a boil. Transfer the chicken to sauce mixture and toss to coat. Garnish with sesame to serve.

Easy Hot Chicken Drumsticks

Servings: 6
Cooking Time: 40 Minutes
Ingredients:
- 6 chicken drumsticks
- Sauce:
- 6 ounces hot sauce
- 3 tablespoons olive oil
- 3 tablespoons tamari sauce
- 1 teaspoon dried thyme
- 1/2 teaspoon dried oregano

Directions:

1. Spritz the sides and bottom of the cooking basket with a nonstick cooking spray.
2. Cook the chicken drumsticks at 380 degrees F for 35 minutes, flipping them over halfway through.
3. Meanwhile, heat the hot sauce, olive oil, tamari sauce, thyme, and oregano in a pan over medium-low heat; reserve.
4. Drizzle the sauce over the prepared chicken drumsticks; toss to coat well and serve. Bon appétit!

Chicken Meatballs

Servings: 10
Cooking Time: 20 Minutes
Ingredients:
- 2 chicken breasts
- 1 tbsp. mustard powder
- 1 tbsp. cumin
- 1 tbsp. basil
- 1 tbsp. thyme
- 1 tsp. chili powder
- 3 tbsp. soy sauce
- 2 tbsp. honey
- 1 onion, diced
- Pepper and salt to taste

Directions:
1. Blend the chicken in your food processor to make a mince. Place the rest of the ingredients in the processor and pulse to combine well.
2. Shape the mixture into several small meatballs and place each one in the basket of the Air Fryer.
3. Air fry at 350°F for 15 minutes. Serve hot.

Chicken Roast With Pineapple Salsa

Servings: 2
Cooking Time: 45 Minutes
Ingredients:
- ¼ cup extra virgin olive oil
- ¼ cup freshly chopped cilantro
- 1 avocado, diced
- 1-pound boneless chicken breasts

- 2 cups canned pineapples
- 2 teaspoons honey
- Juice from 1 lime
- Salt and pepper to taste

Directions:

1. Preheat the air fryer to 390F.
2. Place the grill pan accessory in the air fryer.
3. Season the chicken breasts with lime juice, olive oil, honey, salt, and pepper.
4. Place on the grill pan and cook for 45 minutes.
5. Flip the chicken every 10 minutes to grill all sides evenly.
6. Once the chicken is cooked, serve with pineapples, cilantro, and avocado.

Grilled Chicken Pesto

Servings: 8
Cooking Time: 30 Minutes

Ingredients:

- 1 ¾ cup commercial pesto
- 8 chicken thighs
- Salt and pepper to taste

Directions:

1. Place all Ingredients in the Ziploc bag and allow to marinate in the fridge for at least 2 hours.
2. Preheat the air fryer to 390F.
3. Place the grill pan accessory in the air fryer.
4. Grill the chicken for at least 30 minutes.
5. Make sure to flip the chicken every 10 minutes for even grilling.

Honey Glazed Turkey Breast

Servings: 6
Cooking Time: 55 Minutes

Ingredients:

- 2 tsp. butter, softened
- 1 tsp. dried sage
- 2 sprigs rosemary, chopped
- 1 tsp. salt
- ¼ tsp. freshly ground black pepper, or more if desired

- 1 whole turkey breast
- 2 tbsp. turkey broth
- ¼ cup honey
- 2 tbsp. whole-grain mustard
- 1 tbsp. butter

Directions:

1. Pre-heat your Air Fryer to 360°F.
2. Mix together the 2 tbsp. of butter, sage, rosemary, salt, and pepper.
3. Rub the turkey breast with this mixture.
4. Place the turkey in your fryer's cooking basket and roast for 20 minutes. Turn the turkey breast over and allow to cook for another 15 - 16 minutes.
5. Finally turn it once more and roast for another 12 minutes.
6. In the meantime, mix together the remaining ingredients in a saucepan using a whisk.
7. Coat the turkey breast with the glaze.
8. Place the turkey back in the Air Fryer and cook for an additional 5 minutes. Remove it from the fryer, let it rest, and carve before serving.

Chicken Cheesy Divan Casserole

Servings: 3
Cooking Time: 45 Minutes

Ingredients:

- Salt and pepper to taste
- 1 cup shredded Cheddar cheese
- 1 broccoli head
- ½ cup mushroom soup cream
- ½ cup croutons

Directions:

1. Preheat the air fryer to 390 F. Place the chicken breasts on a clean flat surface and season with salt and pepper. Grease with cooking spray and place them in the fryer basket. Close the air fryer and cook for 13 minutes. Meanwhile, place the broccoli on the chopping board and use a knife to chop.
2. Remove them onto the chopping board, let cool, and cut into bite-size pieces. In a bowl, add the chicken, broccoli, cheddar cheese, and mushroom soup cream; mix well. Scoop the mixture into a 3 X

3cm casserole dish, add the croutons on top and spray with cooking spray. Put the dish in the basket and cook for 10 minutes. Serve with a side of steamed greens.

Italian-style Spicy Chicken Breasts

Servings: 4
Cooking Time: 20 Minutes
Ingredients:
- 2 ounces Asiago cheese, cut into sticks
- 1/3 cup tomato paste
- 1/2 teaspoon garlic paste
- 2 chicken breasts, cut in half lengthwise
- 1/2 cup green onions, chopped
- 1 tablespoon chili sauce
- 1/2 cup roasted vegetable stock
- 1 tablespoon sesame oil
- 1 teaspoon salt
- 2 teaspoons unsweetened cocoa
- 1/2 teaspoon sweet paprika, or more to taste

Directions:
1. Sprinkle chicken breasts with the salt and sweet paprika; drizzle with chili sauce. Now, place a stick of Asiago cheese in the middle of each chicken breast.
2. Then, tie the whole thing using a kitchen string; give a drizzle of sesame oil.
3. Transfer the stuffed chicken to the cooking basket. Add the other ingredients and toss to coat the chicken.
4. Afterward, cook for about 11 minutes at 395 degrees F. Serve the chicken on two serving plates, garnish with fresh or pickled salad and serve immediately. Bon appétit!

Easy Turkey Breasts With Basil

Servings: 4
Cooking Time: 1 Hour
Ingredients:
- 2 tablespoons olive oil
- 2 pounds turkey breasts, bone-in skin-on

- Coarse sea salt and ground black pepper, to taste
- 1 teaspoon fresh basil leaves, chopped
- 2 tablespoons lemon zest, grated

Directions:
1. Rub olive oil on all sides of the turkey breasts; sprinkle with salt, pepper, basil, and lemon zest.
2. Place the turkey breasts skin side up on a parchment-lined cooking basket.
3. Cook in the preheated Air Fryer at 330 degrees F for 30 minutes. Now, turn them over and cook an additional 28 minutes.
4. Serve with lemon wedges, if desired. Bon appétit!

Parmesan-crusted Chicken Fingers

Servings: 2
Cooking Time: 30 Minutes
Ingredients:
- 1 tbsp salt
- 1 tbsp black pepper
- 2 cloves garlic, crushed
- 3 tbsp cornstarch
- 4 tbsp breadcrumbs, like flour bread
- 4 tbsp grated Parmesan cheese
- 2 eggs, beaten
- Cooking spray

Directions:
1. Mix salt, garlic, and pepper in a bowl. Add the chicken and stir to coat. Marinate for 1 hour in the fridge.
2. Mix the breadcrumbs with cheese evenly; set aside. Remove the chicken from the fridge, lightly toss in cornstarch, dip in egg and coat them gently in the cheese mixture. Preheat the air fryer to 350 F. Lightly spray the air fryer basket with cooking spray and place the chicken inside; cook for 15 minutes, until nice and crispy. Serve the chicken with a side of vegetable fries and cheese dip. Yum!

Oregano Turkey And Spinach Bowls

Servings: 4
Cooking Time: 25 Minutes

Ingredients:
- 1 pound turkey meat, ground
- Salt and black pepper to the taste
- 2 tablespoons olive oil
- 10 ounces keto tomato sauce
- 1 tablespoon oregano, chopped
- 2 cups spinach

Directions:

1. Heat up a pan that fits your air fryer with the oil over medium heat, add the turkey, oregano, salt and pepper, stir and brown for 5 minutes. Add the tomato sauce, toss, put the pan in the machine and cook at 370 degrees F for 15 minutes. Add spinach, toss, cook for 5 minutes more, divide everything into bowls and serve.

Cumin Turkey And Celery

Servings: 4

Cooking Time: 30 Minutes

Ingredients:
- 1 big turkey breast, skinless, boneless and sliced
- 4 garlic cloves, minced
- 3 tablespoons olive oil
- 4 celery stalks, roughly chopped
- 1 teaspoon turmeric powder
- 1 teaspoon cumin, ground
- 1 tablespoon smoked paprika
- 1 tablespoon garlic powder

Directions:

1. In a pan that fits the air fryer, combine the turkey and the other ingredients, toss, put the pan in the machine and cook at 380 degrees F for 30 minutes. Divide everything between plates and serve.

Chipotle-garlic Smoked Wings

Servings: 8

Cooking Time: 30 Minutes

Ingredients:
- ½ cup barbecue sauce
- 1 tablespoon chili powder

- 1 tablespoon garlic powder
- 1 tablespoon liquid smoke seasoning
- 1 teaspoon chipotle chili powder
- 1 teaspoon mustard powder
- 3 tablespoons paprika
- 4 pounds chicken wings
- 4 teaspoons salt

Directions:

1. Place all Ingredients in a Ziploc bag
2. Allow to marinate for at least 2 hours in the fridge.
3. Preheat the air fryer to 390F.
4. Place the grill pan accessory in the air fryer.
5. Grill the chicken for 30 minutes.
6. Flip the chicken every 10 minutes for even grilling.
7. Meanwhile, pour the marinade in a saucepan and heat over medium flame until the sauce thickens.
8. Before serving the chicken, brush with the glaze.

Quinoa And Ground Turkey Stuffed Peppers

Servings: 4

Cooking Time: 30 Minutes

Ingredients:
- 1/4 cup canola oil
- 7 ounces ground turkey
- 1/2 cup onion, finely chopped
- 2 cloves garlic, peeled and finely minced
- 1/2 cup quinoa, cooked
- 1 tablespoon fresh cilantro, chopped
- 1 tablespoon fresh parsley, chopped
- 1 ½ cups chopped tomatoes
- 1 teaspoon dried basil
- Salt and black pepper, to taste
- 4 bell peppers, slice off the tops, deveined
- 1/2 cup fat-free chicken broth
- 1 tablespoon cider vinegar
- 1/3 cup shredded three-cheese blend

Directions:

1. Preheat the oil in a saucepan over a moderate heat. Now, sauté the turkey, onion and garlic for 4 to 5 minutes or until they have softened.
2. Add cooked quinoa, cilantro, parsley, 1 cup of tomatoes, basil, salt, and black pepper.
3. Stuff the peppers with the prepared meat filling. Transfer them to a baking dish.
4. After that, thoroughly combine the remaining tomatoes with chicken broth and cider vinegar. Add the sauce to the baking dish.
5. Cook covered at 360 degrees F for 18 minutes. Uncover, top with cheese and cook for 5 minutes more or until cheese is bubbling. Serve right away.

Oregano-thyme Rubbed Thighs

Servings: 4
Cooking Time: 11 Minutes
Ingredients:
- 4 bone-in chicken thighs with skin
- 1/8 teaspoon garlic salt
- 1/8 teaspoon onion salt
- 1/8 teaspoon dried oregano
- 1/8 teaspoon ground thyme
- 1/8 teaspoon paprika
- 1/8 teaspoon ground black pepper

Directions:
1. Lightly grease baking pan of air fryer with cooking spray. Place chicken with skin side touching the bottom of pan.
2. In a small bowl whisk well pepper, paprika, thyme, oregano, onion salt, and garlic salt. Sprinkle all over chicken.
3. For 1 minute, cook on 390F.
4. Turnover chicken while rubbing on bottom and sides of pan for more seasoning.
5. Cook for 10 minutes at 390F.
6. Serve and enjoy.

Buffalo Style Chicken Dip

Servings: 4
Cooking Time: 20 Minutes

Ingredients:
- 1 (8 ounce) package cream cheese, softened
- 1 tablespoon shredded pepper Jack cheese
- 1/2 pinch cayenne pepper, for garnish
- 1/2 pinch cayenne pepper, or to taste
- 1/4 cup and 2 tablespoons hot pepper sauce
- 1/4 cup blue cheese dressing
- 1/4 cup crumbled blue cheese
- 1/4 cup shredded pepper Jack cheese
- 1/4 teaspoon seafood seasoning
- 1-1/2 cups diced cooked rotisserie chicken

Directions:
1. Lightly grease baking pan of air fryer with cooking spray. Mix in cayenne pepper, seafood seasoning, crumbled blue cheese, blue cheese dressing, pepper Jack, hot pepper sauce, cream cheese, and chicken.
2. For 15 minutes, cook on 390F.
3. Let it stand for 5 minutes and garnish with cayenne pepper.
4. Serve and enjoy.

Chinese Five Spiced Marinated Chicken

Servings: 4
Cooking Time: 40 Minutes
Ingredients:
- ¼ cup hoisin sauce
- 1 ¼ teaspoons sesame oil
- 1 ½ teaspoon five spice powder
- 2 chicken breasts, halved
- 2 tablespoons rice vinegar
- 2 teaspoons brown sugar
- 3 ½ teaspoon grated ginger
- 3 ½ teaspoons honey
- 3 cucumbers, sliced
- Salt and pepper to taste

Directions:
1. Place all Ingredients except for the cucumber in a Ziploc bag.
2. Allow to rest in the fridge for at least 2 hours.
3. Preheat the air fryer to 390F.
4. Place the grill pan accessory in the air fryer.

5. Grill for 40 minutes and make sure to flip the chicken often for even cooking.
6. Serve chicken with cucumber once cooked.

Duck And Coconut Milk Mix

Servings: 4
Cooking Time: 25 Minutes
Ingredients:
- 3 garlic cloves, minced
- 4 duck breasts, boneless, skin-on and scored
- 2 tablespoons olive oil
- ¼ teaspoon coriander, ground
- 14 ounces coconut milk
- Salt and black pepper to the taste
- 1 cup basil, chopped

Directions:
1. Heat up a pan that fits your air fryer with the oil over medium heat, add the duck breasts, skin side down and sear for 5 minutes. Add the rest of the ingredients, toss, put the pan in the fryer and cook at 380 degrees F for 20 minutes. Divide between plates and serve.

Mac's Chicken Nuggets

Servings: 4
Cooking Time: 40 Minutes
Ingredients:
- 2 slices friendly breadcrumbs
- 9 oz. chicken breast, chopped
- 1 tsp. garlic, minced
- 1 tsp. tomato ketchup
- 2 medium egg
- 1 tbsp. olive oil
- 1 tsp. paprika
- 1 tsp. parsley
- Salt and pepper to taste

Directions:
1. Combine the breadcrumbs, paprika, salt, pepper and oil into a thick batter.

2. Coat the chopped chicken with the parsley, one egg and ketchup.
3. Shape the mixture into several nuggets and dredge each one in the other egg. Roll the nuggets into the breadcrumbs.
4. Cook at 390°F for 10 minutes in the Air Fryer.
5. Serve the nuggets with a side of mayo dip if desired.

Chicken Enchiladas

Servings: 6
Cooking Time: 65 Minutes
Ingredients:
- 2 cups cheese, grated
- ½ cup salsa
- 1 can green chilies, chopped
- 12 flour tortillas
- 2 cans enchilada sauce

Directions:
1. Preheat your Fryer to 400 F. In a bowl, mix salsa and enchilada sauce. Toss in the chopped chicken to coat. Place the chicken on the tortillas and roll; top with cheese. Place the prepared tortillas in the air fryer cooking basket and cook for 60 minutes. Serve with guacamole

Spicy Chicken And Tomato Sauce

Servings: 8
Cooking Time: 18 Minutes
Ingredients:
- 8 chicken drumsticks
- ½ teaspoon cayenne pepper
- ½ teaspoon chili powder
- ¼ teaspoon jalapeno pepper, minced
- ½ teaspoon ground cumin
- 1 teaspoon dried thyme
- 1 teaspoon keto tomato sauce
- 1 tablespoon nut oil
- ½ teaspoon salt

Directions:

1. In the mixing bowl mix up tomato sauce and nut oil. Then add minced jalapeno pepper and stir the mixture until homogenous. Rub the chicken drumsticks with chili powder, cayenne pepper, dried cumin, thyme, and sprinkle with salt. Then brush the chicken with tomato sauce mixture and leave to marinate for overnight or for at least 8 hours. Preheat the air fryer to 375F. Put the marinated chicken drumsticks in the air fryer and cook them for 18 minutes.

Air Fried Crispy Chicken Tenders

Servings: 3
Cooking Time: 30 Minutes
Ingredients:
- 2 (6-ounces) boneless, skinless chicken breasts, pounded into ½-inch thickness and cut into tenders
- ½ cup all-purpose flour
- 1½ cups panko breadcrumbs
- ¼ cup Parmesan cheese, finely grated
- 2 large eggs
- 1½ teaspoons Worcestershire sauce, divided
- ¾ cup buttermilk
- ½ teaspoon smoked paprika, divided
- Salt and ground black pepper, as required

Directions:
1. Preheat the Air fryer to 400F and grease an Air fryer basket.
2. Mix buttermilk, ¾ teaspoon of Worcestershire sauce, ¼ teaspoon of paprika, salt, and black pepper in a bowl.
3. Combine the flour, remaining paprika, salt, and black pepper in another bowl.
4. Whisk the egg and remaining Worcestershire sauce in a third bowl.
5. Mix the panko breadcrumbs and Parmesan cheese in a fourth bowl.
6. Put the chicken tenders into the buttermilk mixture and refrigerate overnight.
7. Remove the chicken tenders from the buttermilk mixture and dredge into the flour mixture.

8. Dip into the egg and coat with the breadcrumb mixture.
9. Arrange half of the chicken tenders into the Air Fryer basket and cook for about 15 minutes, flipping once in between.
10. Repeat with the remaining mixture and dish out to serve hot.

Cheddar Garlic Turkey

Servings: 4
Cooking Time: 20 Minutes
Ingredients:
- 1 big turkey breast, skinless, boneless and cubed
- Salt and black pepper to the taste
- ¼ cup cheddar cheese, grated
- ¼ teaspoon garlic powder
- 1 tablespoon olive oil

Directions:
1. Rub the turkey cubes with the oil, season with salt, pepper and garlic powder and dredge in cheddar cheese. Put the turkey bits in your air fryer's basket and cook at 380 degrees F for 20 minutes. Divide between plates and serve with a side salad.

Sausage, Ham And Hash Brown Bake

Servings: 4
Cooking Time: 45 Minutes
Ingredients:
- 1/2 pound chicken sausages, smoked
- 1/2 pound ham, sliced
- 6 ounces hash browns, frozen and shredded
- 2 garlic cloves, minced
- 8 ounces spinach
- 1/2 cup Ricotta cheese
- 1/2 cup Asiago cheese, grated
- 4 eggs
- 1/2 cup yogurt
- 1/2 cup milk
- Salt and ground black pepper, to taste
- 1 teaspoon smoked paprika

Directions:

1. Start by preheating your Air Fryer to 380 degrees F. Cook the sausages and ham for 10 minutes; set aside.

2. Meanwhile, in a preheated saucepan, cook the hash browns and garlic for 4 minutes, stirring frequently; remove from the heat, add the spinach and cover with the lid.

3. Allow the spinach to wilt completely. Transfer the sautéed mixture to a baking pan. Add the reserved sausage and ham.

4. In a mixing dish, thoroughly combine the cheese, eggs, yogurt, milk, salt, pepper, and paprika. Pour the cheese mixture over the hash browns in the pan.

5. Place the baking pan in the cooking basket and cook approximately 30 minutes or until everything is thoroughly cooked. Bon appétit!

Cheese Herb Chicken Wings

Servings: 4
Cooking Time: 15 Minutes
Ingredients:

- 2 lbs chicken wings
- 1 tsp herb de Provence
- ½ cup parmesan cheese, grated
- 1 tsp paprika
- Salt

Directions:

1. Preheat the air fryer to 350 F.

2. In a small bowl, mix together cheese, herb de Provence, paprika, and salt.

3. Spray air fryer basket with cooking spray.

4. Toss chicken wings with cheese mixture and place into the air fryer basket and cook for 15 minutes. Turn halfway through.

5. Serve and enjoy.

Spanish Chicken With Golden Potatoes

Servings: 4
Cooking Time: 25 Minutes
Ingredients:

- 2 tablespoons butter, melted
- 4 chicken drumsticks, bone-in
- 1 pound Yukon Gold potatoes, peeled and diced
- 1 lemon, 1/2 juiced, 1/2 cut into wedges
- 1 teaspoon fresh garlic, minced
- 1 teaspoon dried rosemary, crushed
- 1 teaspoon dried thyme, crushed
- 1 teaspoon cayenne pepper
- 1/3 teaspoon freshly ground black pepper
- Kosher salt, to taste
- 2 tablespoons sherry

Directions:

1. Start by preheating your Air Fryer to 370 degrees F. Then, grease a baking pan with the melted butter. Arrange the chicken drumsticks in the baking pan.

2. Bake in the preheated Air Fryer for 8 minutes. Add the diced potatoes. Drizzle chicken and potatoes with lemon juice. Sprinkle with garlic, rosemary, thyme, cayenne pepper, black pepper, and salt.

3. Turn the temperature to 400 degrees F and cook for a further 12 minutes. Make sure to shake the basket once or twice.

4. Remove from the Air Fryer basket and sprinkle sherry on top. Serve with the lemon wedges.

5. Enjoy!

Chicken With Carrots

Servings: 2
Cooking Time: 25 Minutes
Ingredients:

- 1 carrot, peeled and thinly sliced
- 2 tablespoons butter
- 2 (4-ounces) chicken breast halves
- 1 tablespoon fresh rosemary, chopped
- Salt and black pepper, as required
- 2 tablespoons fresh lemon juice

Directions:

1. Preheat the Air fryer to 375F and grease an Air fryer basket.

2. Place 2 square-shaped parchment papers onto a smooth surface and arrange carrot slices evenly in the center of each parchment paper.

3. Drizzle ½ tablespoon of butter over carrot slices and season with salt and black pepper.

4. Layer with chicken breasts and top with rosemary, lemon juice and remaining butter.

5. Fold the parchment paper on all sides and transfer into the Air fryer.

6. Cook for about 25 minutes and dish out in a serving platter to serve.

Sweet And Sour Chicken Thighs

Servings: 2

Cooking Time: 20 Minutes

Ingredients:

- 1 scallion, finely chopped
- 2 (4-ounces) skinless, boneless chicken thighs
- ½ cup corn flour
- 1 garlic clove, minced
- ½ tablespoon soy sauce
- ½ tablespoon rice vinegar
- 1 teaspoon sugar
- Salt and black pepper, as required

Directions:

1. Preheat the Air fryer to 390F and grease an Air fryer basket.

2. Mix all the ingredients except chicken and corn flour in a bowl.

3. Place the corn flour in another bowl.

4. Coat the chicken thighs into the marinade and then dredge into the corn flour.

5. Arrange the chicken thighs into the Air Fryer basket, skin side down and cook for about 10 minutes.

6. Set the Air fryer to 355F and cook for 10 more minutes.

7. Dish out the chicken thighs onto a serving platter and serve hot.

Italian-style Chicken With Roma Tomatoes

Servings: 8

Cooking Time: 45 Minutes

Ingredients:

- 2 teaspoons olive oil, melted
- 3 pounds chicken breasts, bone-in
- 1/2 teaspoon black pepper, freshly ground
- 1/2 teaspoon salt
- 1 teaspoon cayenne pepper
- 2 tablespoons fresh parsley, minced
- 1 teaspoon fresh basil, minced
- 1 teaspoon fresh rosemary, minced
- 4 medium-sized Roma tomatoes, halved

Directions:

1. Start by preheating your Air Fryer to 370 degrees F. Brush the cooking basket with 1 teaspoon of olive oil.

2. Sprinkle the chicken breasts with all seasonings listed above.

3. Cook for 25 minutes or until chicken breasts are slightly browned. Work in batches.

4. Arrange the tomatoes in the cooking basket and brush them with the remaining teaspoon of olive oil. Season with sea salt.

5. Cook the tomatoes at 350 degrees F for 10 minutes, shaking halfway through the cooking time. Serve with chicken breasts. Bon appétit!

Herb Seasoned Turkey Breast

Servings: 4

Cooking Time: 35 Minutes

Ingredients:

- 2 lbs turkey breast
- 1 tsp fresh sage, chopped
- 1 tsp fresh rosemary, chopped
- 1 tsp fresh thyme, chopped
- Pepper
- Salt

Directions:

1. Spray air fryer basket with cooking spray.

2. In a small bowl, mix together sage, rosemary, and thyme.

3. Season turkey breast with pepper and salt and rub with herb mixture.

4. Place turkey breast in air fryer basket and cook at 390 F for 30-35 minutes.

5. Slice and serve.

Chicken Wrapped In Bacon

Servings: 6

Cooking Time: 25 Minutes

Ingredients:

- 6 rashers unsmoked back bacon
- 1 small chicken breast
- 1 tbsp. garlic soft cheese

Directions:

1. Cut the chicken breast into six bite-sized pieces.

2. Spread the soft cheese across one side of each slice of bacon.

3. Put the chicken on top of the cheese and wrap the bacon around it, holding it in place with a toothpick.

4. Transfer the wrapped chicken pieces to the Air Fryer and cook for 15 minutes at 350°F.

Gourmet Chicken Omelet

Servings: 2

Cooking Time: 15 Minutes

Ingredients:

- 4 eggs, whisked
- 4 oz. ground chicken
- ½ cup scallions, finely chopped
- 2 cloves garlic, finely minced
- ½ tsp. salt
- ½ tsp. ground black pepper
- ½ tsp. paprika
- 1 tsp. dried thyme
- Dash of hot sauce

Directions:

1. Mix together all the ingredients in a bowl, ensuring to incorporate everything well.

2. Lightly grease two oven-safe ramekins with vegetable oil. Divide the mixture between them.

3. Transfer them to the Air Fryer, and air fry at 350°F for 13 minutes.

4. Ensure they are cooked through and serve immediately.

Randy's Roasted Chicken

Servings: 4

Cooking Time: 55 Minutes

Ingredients:

- 5 – 7 lb. whole chicken with skin
- 1 tsp. garlic powder
- 1 tsp. onion powder
- ½ tsp. dried thyme
- ½ tsp. dried basil
- ½ tsp. dried rosemary
- ½ tsp. black pepper
- 2 tsp. salt
- 2 tbsp. extra virgin olive oil

Directions:

1. Massage the salt, pepper, herbs, and olive oil into the chicken. Allow to marinade for a minimum of 20 – 30 minutes.

2. In the meantime, pre-heat the Air Fryer to 340 F.

3. Place the chicken in the fryer and cook for 18 – 20 minutes.

4. Flip the chicken over and cook for an additional 20 minutes.

5. Leave the chicken to rest for about 10 minutes before carving and serving.

Coriander Chicken Breast

Servings: 5

Cooking Time: 20 Minutes

Ingredients:

- 15 oz chicken breast, skinless, boneless
- 1 teaspoon lemongrass
- 1 teaspoon ground black pepper
- 1 teaspoon salt

- 1 teaspoon chili powder
- 1 teaspoon smoked paprika
- 2 teaspoons apple cider vinegar
- 1 teaspoon lemon juice
- 1 tablespoon sunflower oil
- 1 teaspoon dried basil
- ½ teaspoon ground coriander
- 2 tablespoons water
- 1 tablespoon heavy cream

Directions:

1. Make the marinade: In the bowl mix up lemongrass, ground black pepper, salt, chili powder, smoked paprika, apple cider vinegar, lemon juice, sunflower oil, dried basil, ground coriander, water, and heavy cream. Then chop the chicken breast roughly and put it in the marinade. Stir it well and leave for 20 minutes in the fridge. Then preheat the air fryer to 375F. Put the marinated chicken breast pieces in the air fryer and cook them for 20 minutes. Shake the chicken pieces after 10 minutes of cooking to avoid burning. The cooked chicken breast pieces should have a light brown color.

Bbq Pineapple 'n Teriyaki Glazed Chicken

Servings: 4

Cooking Time: 23 Minutes

Ingredients:

- ¼ cup pineapple juice
- ¼ teaspoon pepper
- ½ cup brown sugar
- ½ cup soy sauce
- ½ teaspoon salt
- 1 green bell pepper, cut into 1-inch cubes
- 1 red bell pepper, cut into 1-inch cubes
- 1 red onion, cut into 1-inch cubes
- 1 Tablespoon cornstarch
- 1 Tablespoon water
- 1 yellow red bell pepper, cut into 1-inch cubes
- 2 boneless skinless chicken breasts, cut into 1-inch cubes
- 2 cups fresh pineapple cut into 1-inch cubes

- 2 garlic cloves, minced
- green onions, for garnish

Directions:

1. In a saucepan, bring to a boil salt, pepper, garlic, pineapple juice, soy sauce, and brown sugar. In a small bowl whisk well, cornstarch and water. Slowly stir in to mixture in pan while whisking constantly. Simmer until thickened, around 3 minutes. Save ¼ cup of the sauce for basting and set aside.

2. In shallow dish, mix well chicken and remaining thickened sauce. Toss well to coat. Marinate in the ref for a half hour.

3. Thread bell pepper, onion, pineapple, and chicken pieces in skewers. Place on skewer rack in air fryer.

4. For 10 minutes, cook on 360F. Halfway through cooking time, turnover skewers and baste with sauce. If needed, cook in batches.

5. Serve and enjoy with a sprinkle of green onions.

Tender Buttermilk Chicken

Servings: 4

Cooking Time: 1 Hour 20 Minutes

Ingredients:

- 3/4 cup of buttermilk
- 1 ½ pounds chicken tenders
- 1/2 cup coconut flour
- 2 tablespoons flaxseed meal
- Salt, to your liking
- 1/2 teaspoon pink peppercorns, freshly cracked
- 1 teaspoon shallot powder
- 1/2 teaspoon cumin powder
- 1 ½ teaspoon smoked cayenne pepper
- 1 tablespoon sesame oil

Directions:

1. Place the buttermilk and chicken tenders in the mixing dish; gently stir to coat and let it soak for 1 hour.

2. Then, mix the coconut flour with flaxseed meal and all seasonings. Coat the soaked chicken tenders with the coconut flour mixture; now, dip them into the buttermilk.

3. Finally, dredge them in the coconut flour mixture.

4. Brush the prepared chicken tenders with sesame oil and lower them onto the bottom of a cooking basket.

5. Air-fry for 15 minutes at 365 degrees F; make sure to shake them once or twice. Bon appétit!

Rosemary Lemon Chicken

Servings: 2
Cooking Time: 60 Minutes
Ingredients:
- 1 tbsp minced ginger
- 2 rosemary sprigs
- ½ lemon, cut into wedges
- 1 tbsp soy sauce
- ½ tbsp olive oil
- 1 tbsp oyster sauce
- 3 tbsp brown sugar

Directions:
1. Add the ginger, soy sauce, and olive oil, in a bowl; add the chicken and coat well. Cover the bowl and refrigerate for 30 minutes. Preheat the air fryer to 370 F. Transfer the marinated chicken to a baking dish; cook for 6 minutes. Mix oyster sauce, rosemary, and brown sugar in a bowl. Pour the sauce over the chicken. Arrange the lemon wedges in the dish. Return to the air fryer and cook for 13 minutes.

Gingered Chicken Drumsticks

Servings: 3
Cooking Time: 25 Minutes
Ingredients:
- ¼ cup full-fat coconut milk
- 3 (6-ounces) chicken drumsticks
- 2 teaspoons fresh ginger, minced
- 2 teaspoons galangal, minced
- 2 teaspoons ground turmeric
- Salt, to taste

Directions:

1. Preheat the Air fryer to 375F and grease an Air fryer basket.

2. Mix the coconut milk, galangal, ginger, and spices in a bowl.

3. Add the chicken drumsticks and coat generously with the marinade.

4. Refrigerate to marinate for at least 8 hours and transfer into the Air fryer basket.

5. Cook for about 25 minutes and dish out the chicken drumsticks onto a serving platter.

Goulash

Servings: 2
Cooking Time: 20 Minutes
Ingredients:
- 2 chopped bell peppers
- 2 diced tomatoes
- 1 lb. ground chicken
- ½ cup chicken broth
- Salt and pepper

Directions:
1. Pre-heat your fryer at 365°F and spray with cooking spray.

2. Cook the bell pepper for five minutes.

3. Add in the diced tomatoes and ground chicken. Combine well, then allow to cook for a further six minutes.

4. Pour in chicken broth, and season to taste with salt and pepper. Cook for another six minutes before serving.

Old-fashioned Chicken Drumettes

Servings: 3
Cooking Time: 30 Minutes
Ingredients:
- 1/3 cup all-purpose flour
- 1/2 teaspoon ground white pepper
- 1 teaspoon seasoning salt
- 1 teaspoon garlic paste
- 1 teaspoon rosemary
- 1 whole egg + 1 egg white
- 6 chicken drumettes

24

- 1 heaping tablespoon fresh chives, chopped

Directions:

1. Start by preheating your Air Fryer to 390 degrees.
2. Mix the flour with white pepper, salt, garlic paste, and rosemary in a small-sized bowl.
3. In another bowl, beat the eggs until frothy.
4. Dip the chicken into the flour mixture, then into the beaten eggs; coat with the flour mixture one more time.
5. Cook the chicken drumettes for 22 minutes. Serve warm, garnished with chives.

Sesame Chicken Mix

Servings: 4

Cooking Time: 20 Minutes

Ingredients:

- 2 pounds chicken breasts, skinless, boneless and cubed
- ½ cup yellow onion, chopped
- Salt and black pepper to taste
- 1 tablespoon olive oil
- 2 garlic cloves, minced
- ½ cup soy sauce
- 2 teaspoons sesame oil
- ½ cup honey
- ¼ teaspoon red pepper flakes
- 1 tablespoon sesame seeds, toasted

Directions:

1. Heat up the oil in a pan that fits your air fryer oil over medium heat.
2. Add the chicken, toss, and brown for 3 minutes.
3. Add the onions, garlic, salt, and pepper; stir, and cook for 2 minutes more.
4. Add the soy sauce, sesame oil, honey, and pepper flakes; toss well.
5. Place the pan in the fryer and cook at 380 degrees F for 15 minutes.
6. Top with the sesame seeds and toss.
7. Divide between plates and serve.

Cumin Chicken Wings

Servings: 6

Cooking Time: 31 Minutes

Ingredients:

- 12 chicken wings
- 1/2 tsp turmeric
- 2 tsp cumin seeds
- 1 garlic clove, minced
- 3 tbsp ghee
- 1/2 tsp pepper
- 1/2 tsp salt

Directions:

1. Preheat the air fryer to 400 F.
2. In a large bowl, mix together 1 teaspoon cumin, 1 tbsp ghee, turmeric, pepper, and salt.
3. Add chicken wings to the bowl and toss until well coated.
4. Add chicken wings into the air fryer basket and cook for 24 minutes. Shake basket halfway through.
5. Turn chicken wings to another side and cook for 5 minutes more.
6. Meanwhile, heat remaining ghee in a pan over medium heat.
7. Once the ghee is melted add garlic and cumin and cook for a minute. Remove pan from heat and set aside.
8. Remove chicken wings from air fryer and spoon ghee mixture over each chicken wing.
9. Cook chicken wings 2-3 minutes more.
10. Serve and enjoy.

Duck Breasts With Candy Onion And Coriander

Servings: 4

Cooking Time: 25 Minutes

Ingredients:

- 1 ½ pounds duck breasts, skin removed
- 1 teaspoon kosher salt
- 1/2 teaspoon cayenne pepper
- 1/3 teaspoon black pepper
- 1/2 teaspoon smoked paprika
- 1 tablespoon Thai red curry paste
- 1 cup candy onions, halved

- 1/4 small pack coriander, chopped

Directions:

1. Place the duck breasts between 2 sheets of foil; then, use a rolling pin to bash the duck until they are 1-inch thick.
2. Preheat your Air Fryer to 395 degrees F.
3. Rub the duck breasts with salt, cayenne pepper, black pepper, paprika, and red curry paste. Place the duck breast in the cooking basket.
4. Cook for 11 to 12 minutes. Top with candy onions and cook for another 10 to 11 minutes.
5. Serve garnished with coriander and enjoy! .

Italian Chicken And Cheese Frittata

Servings: 4
Cooking Time: 25 Minutes
Ingredients:

- 1 (1-pound) fillet chicken breast
- Sea salt and ground black pepper, to taste
- 1 tablespoon olive oil
- 4 eggs
- 1/2 teaspoon cayenne pepper
- 1/2 cup Mascarpone cream
- 1/4 cup Asiago cheese, freshly grated

Directions:

1. Flatten the chicken breast with a meat mallet. Season with salt and pepper.
2. Heat the olive oil in a frying pan over medium flame. Cook the chicken for 10 to 12 minutes; slice into small strips, and reserve.
3. Then, in a mixing bowl, thoroughly combine the eggs, and cayenne pepper; season with salt to taste. Add the cheese and stir to combine.
4. Add the reserved chicken. Then, pour the mixture into a lightly greased pan; put the pan into the cooking basket.
5. Cook in the preheated Air Fryer at 355 degrees F for 10 minutes, flipping over halfway through.

Chicken And Squash

Servings: 4
Cooking Time: 25 Minutes
Ingredients:

- 3 garlic cloves, minced
- 2 tablespoons olive oil
- 2 red chilies, minced
- 2 tablespoons green curry paste
- A pinch of cumin, ground
- ¼ teaspoon coriander, ground
- 14 ounces coconut milk
- 6 cups squash, cubed
- 8 chicken drumsticks
- Salt and black pepper to taste
- ½ cup cilantro, chopped
- ½ cup basil, chopped

Directions:

1. Heat up a pan that fits your air fryer with the oil over medium heat.
2. Add the garlic, chilies, curry paste, cumin, coriander, salt, and pepper; stir, and cook for 3-4 minutes.
3. Add the chicken pieces and the coconut milk, and stir.
4. Place the pan in the fryer and cook at 380 degrees F for 15 minutes.
5. Add the squash, cilantro, and basil; toss, and cook for 5-6 minutes more.
6. Divide into bowls and serve. Enjoy!

Thai Chicken With Bacon

Servings: 2
Cooking Time: 50 Minutes
Ingredients:

- 4 rashers smoked bacon
- 2 chicken filets
- 1/2 teaspoon coarse sea salt
- 1/4 teaspoon black pepper, preferably freshly ground
- 1 teaspoon garlic, minced
- 1 (2-inch) piece ginger, peeled and minced
- 1 teaspoon black mustard seeds
- 1 teaspoon mild curry powder
- 1/2 cup coconut milk
- 1/2 cup parmesan cheese, grated

Directions:

1. Start by preheating your Air Fryer to 400 degrees F. Add the smoked bacon and cook in the preheated Air Fryer for 5 to 7 minutes. Reserve.

2. In a mixing bowl, place the chicken fillets, salt, black pepper, garlic, ginger, mustard seeds, curry powder, and milk. Let it marinate in your refrigerator about 30 minutes.

3. In another bowl, place the grated parmesan cheese.

4. Dredge the chicken fillets through the parmesan mixture and transfer them to the cooking basket. Reduce the temperature to 380 degrees F and cook the chicken for 6 minutes.

5. Turn them over and cook for a further 6 minutes. Repeat the process until you have run out of ingredients.

6. Serve with reserved bacon. Enjoy!

Nacho-fried Chicken Burgers

Servings: 4
Cooking Time: 25 Minutes
Ingredients:
- 1 palmful dried basil
- 1/3 cup parmesan cheese, grated
- 2 teaspoons dried marjoram
- 1/3 teaspoon ancho chili powder
- 2 teaspoons dried parsley flakes
- 1/2 teaspoon onion powder
- Toppings, to serve
- 1/3 teaspoon porcini powder
- 1 teaspoon sea salt flakes
- 1 pound chicken meat, ground
- 2 teaspoons cumin powder
- 1/3 teaspoon red pepper flakes, crushed
- 1 teaspoon freshly cracked black pepper

Directions:
1. Generously grease an Air Fryer cooking basket with a thin layer of vegetable oil.

2. In a mixing dish, combine chicken meat with all seasonings. Shape into 4 patties and coat them with grated parmesan cheese.

3. Cook chicken burgers in the preheated Air Fryer for 15 minutes at 345 degrees F, working in batches, flipping them once.

4. Serve with toppings of choice. Bon appétit!

Spicy Buffalo Chicken Wings

Servings: 4
Cooking Time: 35 Minutes
Ingredients:
- ½ cup cayenne pepper sauce
- ½ cup coconut oil
- 1 tbsp Worcestershire sauce
- 1 tbsp kosher salt

Directions:
1. In a mixing cup, combine cayenne pepper sauce, coconut oil, Worcestershire sauce and salt; set aside. Pat the chicken dry and place in the air fryer cooking basket. Cook for 15 minutes at 380 F. Transfer to a plate and drizzle with the prepared sauce. Serve with celery sticks and enjoy!

Homemade Chicken Nuggets

Servings: 4
Cooking Time: 15 Minutes
Ingredients:
- 4 tbsp sour cream
- ½ cup breadcrumbs
- ½ tbsp garlic powder
- ½ tsp cayenne pepper
- Salt and pepper to taste

Directions:
1. In a bowl, add sour cream and place the chicken. Stir well. Mix the breadcrumbs, garlic, cayenne, salt, and black pepper and scatter onto a plate. Roll up the chicken in the breadcrumbs to coat well. Grease the air with oil. Arrange the nuggets in an even layer and cook for 10 minutes on 360 F, turning once.

BEEF,PORK & LAMB RECIPES

Beef & Veggie Kebabs

Servings: 4

Cooking Time: 12 Minutes

Ingredients:

- ¼ cup soy sauce
- ¼ cup olive oil
- 1 tablespoon garlic, minced
- 1 teaspoon brown sugar
- ½ teaspoon ground cumin
- Salt and ground black pepper, as required
- 1 pound sirloin steak, cut into-inch chunks
- 8 ounces baby Bella mushrooms, stems removed
- 1 large bell pepper, seeded and cut into 1-inch pieces
- 1 red onion, cut into 1-inch pieces

Directions:

1. In a bowl, mix together the soy sauce, oil, garlic, brown sugar, cumin, salt, and black pepper.
2. Add the steak cubes and generously coat with marinade.
3. Refrigerate to marinate for about 30 minutes.
4. Thread the steak cubes, mushrooms, bell pepper, and onion onto metal skewers.
5. Set the temperature of Air Fryer to 390 degrees F. Grease an Air Fryer basket.
6. Arrange skewers into the prepared Air Fryer basket.
7. Air Fry for about 10-12 minutes, flipping once halfway through.
8. Remove from Air Fryer and transfer the kebabs onto a platter.
9. Serve hot.

Garlicky Buttered Chops

Servings: 4

Cooking Time: 30 Minutes

Ingredients:

- 1 tablespoons butter, melted
- 2 teaspoons chopped parsley
- 2 teaspoons grated garlic

- 4 pork chops
- Salt and pepper to taste

Directions:

1. Preheat the air fryer to 330F.
2. Place the grill pan accessory in the air fryer.
3. Season the pork chops with the remaining Ingredients.
4. Place on the grill pan and cook for 30 minutes.
5. Flip the pork chops halfway through the cooking time.

Smoked Beef Burgers

Servings: 4

Cooking Time: 20 Minutes

Ingredients:

- 1 ¼ pounds lean ground beef
- 1 tablespoon soy sauce
- 1 teaspoon Dijon mustard
- A few dashes of liquid smoke
- 1 teaspoon shallot powder
- 1 clove garlic, minced
- 1/2 teaspoon cumin powder
- 1/4 cup scallions, minced
- 1/3 teaspoon sea salt flakes
- 1/3 teaspoon freshly cracked mixed peppercorns
- 1 teaspoon celery seeds
- 1 teaspoon parsley flakes

Directions:

1. Mix all of the above ingredients in a bowl; knead until everything is well incorporated.
2. Shape the mixture into four patties. Next, make a shallow dip in the center of each patty to prevent them puffing up during air-frying.
3. Spritz the patties on all sides using a non-stick cooking spray. Cook approximately 12 minutes at 360 degrees F.
4. Check for doneness – an instant read thermometer should read 160 degrees F. Bon appétit!

Herbed Leg Of Lamb

Servings: 5

Cooking Time: 75 Minutes

Ingredients:

- 2 pounds bone-in leg of lamb
- 2 tablespoons olive oil
- Salt and ground black pepper, as required
- 2 fresh rosemary sprigs
- 2 fresh thyme sprigs

Directions:

1. Coat the leg of lamb with oil and sprinkle with salt and black pepper.
2. Wrap the leg of lamb with herb sprigs.
3. Set the temperature of air fryer to 300 degrees F. Grease an air fryer basket.
4. Place leg of lamb into the prepared air fryer basket.
5. Air fry for about 75 minutes.
6. Remove from air fryer and transfer the leg of lamb onto a platter.
7. With a piece of foil, cover the leg of lamb for about 10 minutes before slicing.
8. Cut the leg of lamb into desired size pieces and serve.

Cardamom Lamb Mix

Servings: 2

Cooking Time: 20 Minutes

Ingredients:

- 10 oz lamb sirloin
- 1 oz fresh ginger, sliced
- 2 oz spring onions, chopped
- ¼ teaspoon ground cinnamon
- ½ teaspoon ground cardamom
- ½ teaspoon fennel seeds
- ½ teaspoon chili flakes
- ¼ teaspoon salt
- 1 tablespoon avocado oil

Directions:

1. Put the fresh ginger in the blender. Add onion, ground cardamom, cinnamon, fennel seeds, chili flakes, salt, and avocado oil. Blend the mixture until you get the smooth mass. After this, make the small cuts in the lamb sirloin. Rub the meat with the blended spice mixture and leave it for 20 minutes to marinate. Meanwhile, preheat the air fryer to 350F. Put the marinated lamb sirloin in the air fryer and cook it for 20 minutes. Flip the meat on another side in halfway. Slice the cooked meat.

Salami Rolls With Homemade Mustard Spread

Servings: 4

Cooking Time: 10 Minutes

Ingredients:

- 7 ounces Manchego cheese, grated
- 2/3 pound pork salami, chopped
- 7 ounces canned crescent rolls
- For the Mustard Spread:
- 1 tablespoon sour cream
- 1/3 teaspoon garlic powder
- 1/3 cup mayonnaise
- 2 ½ tablespoons spicy brown mustard
- Salt, to taste

Directions:

1. Start by preheating your air fryer to 325 degrees F. Now, form the crescent rolls into "sheets".
2. Place the chopped Manchego and pork salami in the middle of each dough sheet.
3. Shape the dough into the rolls; bake the rolls for 8 minutes. Then, decrease the temperature and bake at 290 degrees F for 5 more minutes.
4. In the meantime, combine all of the ingredients for the mustard spread. Arrange the warm rolls on a serving platter and serve with the mustard spread on the side. Enjoy!

Ham And Veggie Air Fried Mix Recipe

Servings: 6

Cooking Time: 30 Minutes

Ingredients:

- 1/4 cup butter
- 1/4 cup flour
- 6 oz. sweet peas
- 4 oz. mushrooms; halved
- 3 cups milk
- 1/2 tsp. thyme; dried
- 2 cups ham; chopped
- 1 cup baby carrots

Directions:

1. Heat up a large pan that fits your air fryer with the butter over medium heat, melt it, add flour and whisk well

2. Add milk and, well again and take off heat

3. Add thyme, ham, peas, mushrooms and baby carrots, toss, put in your air fryer and cook at 360 °F, for 20 minutes. Divide everything on plates and serve.

Cajun Sweet-sour Grilled Pork

Servings: 3

Cooking Time: 12 Minutes

Ingredients:

- ¼ cup brown sugar
- 1/4 cup cider vinegar
- 1-lb pork loin, sliced into 1-inch cubes
- 2 tablespoons Cajun seasoning
- 3 tablespoons brown sugar

Directions:

1. In a shallow dish, mix well pork loin, 3 tablespoons brown sugar, and Cajun seasoning. Toss well to coat. Marinate in the ref for 3 hours.

2. In a medium bowl mix well, brown sugar and vinegar for basting.

3. Thread pork pieces in skewers. Baste with sauce and place on skewer rack in air fryer.

4. For 12 minutes, cook on 360F. Halfway through cooking time, turnover skewers and baste with sauce. If needed, cook in batches.

5. Serve and enjoy.

Pork Tenderloin With Bacon And Veggies

Servings: 3

Cooking Time: 28 Minutes

Ingredients:

- 3 potatoes
- ¾ pound frozen green beans
- 6 bacon slices
- 3 (6-ounces) pork tenderloins
- 2 tablespoons olive oil

Directions:

1. Preheat the Air fryer to 390F and grease an Air fryer basket.

2. Wrap 4-6 green beans with one bacon slice and coat the pork tenderloins with olive oil.

3. Pierce the potatoes with a fork and arrange in the Air fryer basket.

4. Cook for about 15 minutes and add the pork tenderloins.

5. Cook for about 6 minutes and dish out in a bowl.

6. Arrange the bean rolls into the Air fryer basket and top with the pork tenderloins.

7. Cook for about 7 minutes and dish out in a platter.

8. Cut each tenderloin into desired size slices to serve alongside the potatoes and green beans rolls.

Cheesy Stuffed Peppers With Ground Pork

Servings: 3

Cooking Time: 30 Minutes

Ingredients:

- 3 bell peppers, stems and seeds removed
- 1 tablespoon olive oil
- 3 scallions, chopped
- 1 teaspoon fresh garlic, minced
- 12 ounces lean pork, ground
- 1/2 teaspoon sea salt
- 1/2 teaspoon black pepper
- 1 tablespoon fish sauce
- 2 ripe tomatoes, pureed
- 3 ounces Monterey Jack cheese, grated

Directions:

1. Cook the peppers in boiling salted water for 4 minutes

2. In a nonstick skillet, heat the olive oil over medium heat. Then, sauté the scallions and garlic until tender and fragrant.

3. Stir in the ground pork and continue sautéing until the pork has browned; drain off the excess fat.

4. Add the salt, black pepper, fish sauce, and 1 pureed tomato; give it a good stir.

5. Divide the filling among the bell peppers. Arrange the peppers in a baking dish lightly greased with cooking oil. Place the remaining tomato puree around the peppers.

6. Bake in the preheated Air Fryer at 380 degrees F for 13 minutes. Top with grated cheese and bake another 6 minutes. Serve warm and enjoy!

Moroccan Lamb And Garlic

Servings: 4
Cooking Time: 30 Minutes
Ingredients:
- 8 lamb cutlets
- A pinch of salt and black pepper
- 4 tablespoons olive oil
- ½ cup mint leaves
- 6 garlic cloves
- 1 tablespoon cumin, ground
- 1 tablespoon coriander seeds
- Zest of 2 lemons, grated
- 3 tablespoons lemon juice

Directions:
1. In a blender, combine all the ingredients except the lamb and pulse well. Rub the lamb cutlets with this mix, place them in your air fryer's basket and cook at 380 degrees F for 15 minutes on each side. Serve with a side salad.

Beef Sausage With Grilled Broccoli

Servings: 4
Cooking Time: 25 Minutes
Ingredients:

- 1 pound beef Vienna sausage
- 1/2 cup mayonnaise
- 1 teaspoon yellow mustard
- 1 tablespoon fresh lemon juice
- 1 teaspoon garlic powder
- 1/4 teaspoon black pepper
- 1 pound broccoli

Directions:
1. Start by preheating your Air Fryer to 380 degrees F. Spritz the grill pan with cooking oil.

2. Cut the sausages into serving sized pieces. Cook the sausages for 15 minutes, shaking the basket occasionally to get all sides browned. Set aside.

3. In the meantime, whisk the mayonnaise with mustard, lemon juice, garlic powder, and black pepper. Toss the broccoli with the mayo mixture.

4. Turn up temperature to 400 degrees F. Cook broccoli for 6 minutes, turning halfway through the cooking time.

5. Serve the sausage with the grilled broccoli on the side. Bon appétit!

Beef Roast In Worcestershire-rosemary

Servings: 6
Cooking Time: 2 Hours
Ingredients:
- 1 onion, chopped
- 1 tablespoon butter
- 1 tablespoon Worcestershire sauce
- 1 teaspoon rosemary
- 1 teaspoon thyme
- 1-pound beef chuck roast
- 2 cloves of garlic, minced
- 2 tablespoons olive oil
- 3 cups water
- 3 stalks of celery, sliced

Directions:
1. Preheat the air fryer for 5 minutes.

2. Place all ingredients in a deep baking dish that will fit in the air fryer.

3. Bake for 2 hours at 350F.

4.   Braise the meat with its sauce every 30 minutes until cooked.

Classic Skirt Steak Strips With Veggies

Servings: 4
Cooking Time: 17 Minutes
Ingredients:
- 1 (12-ounce) skirt steak, cut into thin strips
- ½ pound fresh mushrooms, quartered
- 6-ounce snow peas
- 1 onion, cut into half rings
- ¼ cup olive oil, divided
- 2 tablespoons soy sauce
- 2 tablespoons honey
- Salt and black pepper, to taste

Directions:
1.   Preheat the Air fryer to 390F and grease an Air fryer basket.
2.   Mix 2 tablespoons of oil, soy sauce and honey in a bowl and coat steak strips with this marinade.
3.   Put vegetables, remaining oil, salt and black pepper in another bowl and toss well.
4.   Transfer the steak strips and vegetables in the Air fryer basket and cook for about 17 minutes.
5.   Dish out and serve warm.

Pork Ribs With Red Wine Sauce

Servings: 4
Cooking Time: 25 Minutes + Marinating Time
Ingredients:
- For the Pork Ribs:
- 1 ½ pounds pork ribs
- 2 tablespoons olive oil
- 1/2 teaspoon freshly cracked black peppercorns
- 1/2 teaspoon Hickory-smoked salt
- 1 tablespoon Dijon mustard
- 2 tablespoons coconut aminos
- 2 tablespoons lime juice
- 1 clove garlic, minced
- For the Red Wine Sauce:

- 1 ½ cups beef stock
- 1 cup red wine
- 1 teaspoon balsamic vinegar
- 1/4 teaspoon salt

Directions:
1.   Place all ingredients for the pork ribs in a large-sized mixing dish. Cover and marinate in your refrigerator overnight or at least 3 hours.
2.   Air-fry the pork ribs for 10 minutes at 320 degrees F.
3.   Meanwhile, make the sauce. Add a beef stock to a deep pan that is preheated over a moderate flame; boil until it is reduced by half.
4.   Add the remaining ingredients and increase the temperature to high heat. Let it cook for further 10 minutes or until your sauce is reduced by half.
5.   Serve the pork ribs with red wine sauce. Bon appétit!

Steak Total

Servings: 4
Cooking Time: 30 Minutes
Ingredients:
- 2 lb. rib eye steak
- 1 tbsp. olive oil
- 1 tbsp. steak rub

Directions:
1.   Set the Air Fryer to 400°F and allow to warm for 4 minutes.
2.   Massage the olive oil and steak rub into both sides of the steak.
3.   Put the steak in the fryer's basket and cook for 14 minutes. Turn the steak over and cook on the other side for another 7 minutes.
4.   Serve hot.

Lamb And Scallion Balls

Servings: 4
Cooking Time: 30 Minutes
Ingredients:
- 1 and ½ pounds lamb, ground

- 1 scallion, chopped
- A pinch of salt and black pepper
- ½ cup pine nuts, toasted and chopped
- 1 tablespoon thyme, chopped
- 2 garlic cloves, minced
- 1 tablespoon olive oil
- 1 egg, whisked

Directions:

1. In a bowl, mix the lamb with the rest of the ingredients except the oil, stir well and shape medium meatballs out of this mix. Grease the meatballs with the oil, put them in your air fryer's basket and cook at 380 degrees F for 15 minutes on each side. Divide between plates and serve with a side salad.

Roast Beef With Balsamic-honey Sauce

Servings: 10
Cooking Time: 2 Hours
Ingredients:

- ½ cup balsamic vinegar
- ½ teaspoon red pepper flakes
- 1 cup beef organic beef broth
- 1 tablespoon coconut aminos
- 1 tablespoon honey
- 1 tablespoon Worcestershire sauce
- 3 pounds boneless roast beef
- 4 cloves of garlic, minced
- 4 tablespoons olive oil

Directions:

1. Place all ingredients in a baking dish and make sure that the entire surface of the beef is coated with the spices.
2. Place the baking dish with the bee in the air fryer. Close.
3. Cook for 2 hours at 400F.

Cumin Pork Steak

Servings: 4
Cooking Time: 25 Minutes

Ingredients:

- 16 oz pork steak (4 oz every steak)
- 1 tablespoon sesame oil
- ½ teaspoon ground paprika
- ½ teaspoon ground cumin
- ½ teaspoon salt
- ½ teaspoon dried garlic

Directions:

1. Sprinkle every pork steak with ground paprika, ground cumin, salt, and dried garlic. Then sprinkle the meat with sesame oil. Preheat the air fryer to 400F. Put the pork steak in the air fryer in one layer and cook them for 15 minutes. Then flip the steaks on another side and cook them for 10 minutes more.

Nana's Pork Chops With Cilantro

Servings: 6
Cooking Time: 22 Minutes
Ingredients:

- 1/3 cup pork rinds
- Roughly chopped fresh cilantro, to taste
- 2 teaspoons Cajun seasonings
- Nonstick cooking spray
- 2 eggs, beaten
- 3 tablespoons almond meal
- 1 teaspoon seasoned salt
- Garlic & onion spice blend, to taste
- 6 pork chops
- 1/3 teaspoon freshly cracked black pepper

Directions:

1. Coat the pork chops with Cajun seasonings, salt, pepper, and the spice blend on all sides.
2. Then, add the almond meal to a plate. In a shallow dish, whisk the egg until pale and smooth. Place the pork rinds in the third bowl.
3. Dredge each pork piece in the almond meal; then, coat them with the egg; finally, coat them with the pork rinds. Spritz them with cooking spray on both sides.
4. Now, air-fry pork chops for about 18 minutes at 345 degrees F; make sure to taste for doneness after

first 12 minutes of cooking. Lastly, garnish with fresh cilantro. Bon appétit!

Pork And Asparagus

Servings: 4
Cooking Time: 35 Minutes
Ingredients:

- 2 pounds pork loin, boneless and cubed
- ¾ cup beef stock
- 2 tablespoons olive oil
- 3 tablespoons keto tomato sauce
- 1 pound asparagus, trimmed and halved
- ½ tablespoon oregano, chopped
- Salt and black pepper to the taste

Directions:

1. Heat up a pan that fits your air fryer with the oil over medium heat, add the pork, toss and brown for 5 minutes. Add the rest of the ingredients, toss a bit, put the pan in the fryer and cook at 380 degrees F for 30 minutes. Divide everything between plates and serve.

Beef Short Ribs

Servings: 8
Cooking Time: 16 Minutes
Ingredients:

- 4 pounds bone-in beef short ribs
- 1/3 cup scallions, chopped
- 1 tablespoon fresh ginger, finely grated
- 1 cup low-sodium soy sauce
- ½ cup rice vinegar
- 1 tablespoon Sriracha
- 2 tablespoons brown sugar
- 1 teaspoon ground black pepper

Directions:

1. Preheat the Air fryer to 385F and grease an Air fryer basket.
2. Put the ribs with all other ingredients in a resealable bag and seal the bag.
3. Shake to coat well and refrigerate overnight.

4. Remove the short ribs from resealable bag and arrange in the Air fryer basket in 2 batches.
5. Cook for about 8 minutes, flipping once in between and dish out onto a serving platter.
6. Repeat with the remaining ribs and serve hot.

Mexican Chili Beef Sausage Meatballs

Servings: 4
Cooking Time: 25 Minutes
Ingredients:

- 1 cup green onion, finely minced
- 1/2 teaspoon parsley flakes
- 2 teaspoons onion flakes
- 1 pound chili sausage, crumbled
- 2 tablespoons flaxseed meal
- 3 cloves garlic, finely minced
- 1 teaspoon Mexican oregano
- 1 tablespoon poblano pepper, chopped
- Fine sea salt and ground black pepper, to taste
- ½ tablespoon fresh chopped sage

Directions:

1. Mix all ingredients in a bowl until the mixture has a uniform consistency.
2. Roll into bite-sized balls and transfer them to a baking dish.
3. Cook in the preheated Air Fryer at 345 degrees for 18 minutes. Serve on wooden sticks and enjoy!

Three-pepper Roast Pork Loin

Servings: 6
Cooking Time: 30 Minutes
Ingredients:

- 1 tablespoon olive oil
- 1 pound pork loin
- 1 teaspoon dried basil
- 1/2 teaspoon dried oregano
- 1/4 teaspoon crushed red pepper flakes
- 1 teaspoon dried thyme
- 1/4 teaspoon freshly grated nutmeg

- Sea salt flakes and freshly ground black pepper, to taste
- 1 Pimento chili pepper, deveined and chopped
- 1 Yellow wax pepper, deveined and chopped
- 1 sweet bell pepper, deveined and chopped
- 1 tablespoon peanut butter
- 1/4 cup beef broth
- 1/2 tablespoon whole-grain mustard
- 1 bay leaf

Directions:

1. Lightly grease the inside of an Air Fryer baking dish with a thin layer of olive oil. Then, cut 8 slit down the center of pork (about 3x3". Sprinkle with the seasonings and massage them into the meat to evenly distribute
2. Then, tuck peppers into the slits and transfer the meat to the Air Fryer baking dish. Scatter remaining peppers around the roast.
3. In a mixing dish, whisk the peanut butter, beef broth, and mustard; now, pour broth mixture around the roast.
4. Add the bay leaf and roast the meat for 25 minutes at 390 degrees F; turn the pork over halfway through the roasting time. Bon appétit!

Char-grilled Skirt Steak With Fresh Herbs

Servings: 3
Cooking Time: 30 Minutes
Ingredients:
- 1 ½ pounds skirt steak, trimmed
- 1 tablespoon lemon zest
- 1 tablespoon olive oil
- 2 cups fresh herbs like tarragon, sage, and mint, chopped
- 4 cloves of garlic, minced
- Salt and pepper to taste

Directions:

1. Preheat the air fryer to 390F.
2. Place the grill pan accessory in the air fryer.
3. Season the steak with salt, pepper, lemon zest, herbs, and garlic.
4. Brush with oil.

5. Grill for 15 minutes and if needed cook in batches.

Garlic Pork And Bok Choy

Servings: 4
Cooking Time: 35 Minutes
Ingredients:
- 4 pork chops, boneless
- 1 bok choy head, torn
- 2 cups chicken stock
- 2 tablespoons coconut aminos
- 2 garlic cloves, minced
- A pinch of salt and black pepper
- 2 tablespoons coconut oil, melted

Directions:

1. Heat up a pan that fits the air fryer with the oil over medium-high heat, add the pork chops and brown for 5 minutes. Add the garlic, salt and pepper and cook for another minute. Add the rest of the ingredients except the bok choy and cook at 380 degrees F for 25 minutes. Add the bok choy, cook for 5 minutes more, divide everything between plates and serve.

Italian Pork

Servings: 2
Cooking Time: 50 Minutes
Ingredients:
- 8 oz pork loin
- 1 tablespoon sesame oil
- ½ teaspoon salt
- 1 teaspoon Italian herbs

Directions:

1. In the shallow bowl mix up Italian herbs, salt, and sesame oil. Then brush the pork loin with the Italian herbs mixture and wrap in the foil. Preheat the air fryer to 350F. Put the wrapped pork loin in the air fryer and cook it for 50 minutes. When the time is over, remove the meat from the air fryer and discard the foil. Slice the pork loin into the servings.

Parmesan Meatballs

Servings: 6
Cooking Time: 8 Minutes

Ingredients:

- 10 oz ground beef
- 4 oz ground pork
- 1 tablespoon taco seasoning
- 1 oz Parmesan, grated
- 1 teaspoon dried cilantro
- 1 teaspoon sesame oil

Directions:

1. In the mixing bowl mix up ground beef, ground pork, taco seasonings, and dried cilantro. When the mixture is homogenous, add Parmesan cheese and stir it well. With the help of the scooper make the medium-size meatballs. Preheat the air fryer to 385F. Brush the air fryer basket with sesame oil from inside and put the meatballs. Arrange them in one layer. Cook the meatballs for 8 minutes. Flip them on another side after 4 minutes of cooking.

Beef Tips With Onion

Servings: 2
Cooking Time: 10 Minutes

Ingredients:

- 1 pound top round beef, cut into 1½-inch cubes
- ½ yellow onion, chopped
- 2 tablespoons Worcestershire sauce
- 1 tablespoon avocado oil
- 1 teaspoon onion powder
- 1 teaspoon garlic powder
- Salt and black pepper, to taste

Directions:

1. Preheat the Air fryer to 360F and grease an Air fryer basket.
2. Mix the beef tips, onion, Worcestershire sauce, oil, and spices in a bowl.
3. Arrange the beef mixture in the Air fryer basket and cook for about 10 minutes.

4. Dish out the steak mixture onto serving plates and cut into desired size slices to serve.

Pork Rolls

Servings: 4
Cooking Time: 15 Minutes

Ingredients:

- 1 scallion, chopped
- ¼ cup sun-dried tomatoes, finely chopped
- 2 tablespoons fresh parsley, chopped
- 4 (6-ounces) pork cutlets, pounded slightly
- Salt and black pepper, as required
- 2 teaspoons paprika
- ½ tablespoon olive oil

Directions:

1. Preheat the Air fryer to 390F and grease an Air fryer basket.
2. Mix the scallion, tomatoes, parsley, salt, and black pepper in a bowl.
3. Spread the tomato mixture over each pork cutlet and roll each cutlet, securing with cocktail sticks
4. Coat the outer part of rolls with paprika, salt and black pepper and drizzle with olive oil.
5. Arrange the pork rolls in the Air fryer basket and cook for about 15 minutes.
6. Dish out onto serving plates and serve hot.

Spanish Pinchos Morunos

Servings: 4
Cooking Time: 25 Minutes + Marinating Time

Ingredients:

- 2 pounds center cut loin chop, cut into bite-sized pieces
- 1 teaspoon oregano
- 1/2 teaspoon ground turmeric
- 1/2 teaspoon ground coriander
- 1 teaspoon ground cumin
- 2 teaspoons sweet Spanish paprika
- Sea salt and freshly ground black pepper, to taste

- 2 garlic cloves, minced
- 2 tablespoons extra virgin olive oil
- 1/4 cup dry red wine
- 1 lemon, 1/2 juiced 1/2 wedges

Directions:

1. Mix all ingredients, except the lemon wedges, in a large ceramic dish. Allow it to marinate for 2 hours in your refrigerator.
2. Discard the marinade. Now, thread the pork pieces on to skewers and place them in the cooking basket.
3. Cook in the preheated Air Fryer at 360 degrees F for 15 to 17 minutes, shaking the basket every 5 minutes. Work in batches.
4. Serve immediately garnished with lemon wedges. Bon appétit!

Pork Chops Romano

Servings: 4

Cooking Time: 1 Hour 12 Minutes

Ingredients:

- 3 eggs, well-beaten
- 1 cup Romano cheese, grated
- 2 teaspoons mustard powder
- 1 ½ tablespoons olive oil
- 1/2 tablespoon soy sauce
- 2 tablespoons Worcestershire sauce
- ½ teaspoon dried rosemary
- 4 large-sized pork chops
- ½ teaspoon dried thyme
- 2 teaspoons fennel seeds
- Salt and freshly cracked black pepper, to taste
- 1 teaspoon red pepper flakes, crushed

Directions:

1. Add the pork chops along with olive oil, soy sauce, Worcestershire sauce, and seasonings to a resealable plastic bag. Allow pork chops to marinate for 50 minutes in your refrigerator.
2. Next step, dip the pork chops into the beaten eggs; then, coat the pork chops with Romano cheese on both sides. Press the breading firmly into the pork chops.

3. Cook in the Air Fryer for 18 minutes at 405 degrees F, turning once. Bon appétit!

Beef, Lettuce And Cabbage Salad

Servings: 4

Cooking Time: 25 Minutes

Ingredients:

- 1 pound beef, cubed
- ¼ cup coconut aminos
- 1 tablespoon coconut oil, melted
- 6 ounces iceberg lettuce, shredded
- 2 tablespoons cilantro, chopped
- 2 tablespoons chives, chopped
- 1 zucchini, shredded
- ½ green cabbage head, shredded
- 2 tablespoons almonds, sliced
- 1 tablespoon sesame seeds
- ½ tablespoon white vinegar
- A pinch of salt and black pepper

Directions:

1. Heat up a pan that fits the air fryer with the oil over medium-high heat, add the meat and brown for 5 minutes. Add the aminos, zucchini, cabbage, salt and pepper, toss, put the pan in the fryer and cook at 370 degrees F for 20 minutes. Cool the mix down, transfer to a salad bowl, add the rest of the ingredients, toss well and serve.

Honey Mustard Cheesy Meatballs

Servings: 8

Cooking Time: 15 Minutes

Ingredients:

- 2 onions, chopped
- 1 pound ground beef
- 4 tablespoons fresh basil, chopped
- 2 tablespoons cheddar cheese, grated
- 2 teaspoons garlic paste
- 2 teaspoons honey
- Salt and black pepper, to taste
- 2 teaspoons mustard

Directions:

1. Preheat the Air fryer to 385F and grease an Air fryer basket.
2. Mix all the ingredients in a bowl until well combined.
3. Shape the mixture into equal-sized balls gently and arrange the meatballs in the Air fryer basket.
4. Cook for about 15 minutes and dish out to serve warm.

Grilled Prosciutto Wrapped Fig

Servings: 2
Cooking Time: 8 Minutes
Ingredients:

- 2 whole figs, sliced in quarters
- 8 prosciutto slices
- Pepper and salt to taste

Directions:

1. Wrap a prosciutto slice around one slice of fid and then thread into skewer. Repeat process for remaining Ingredients. Place on skewer rack in air fryer.
2. For 8 minutes, cook on 390F. Halfway through cooking time, turnover skewers.
3. Serve and enjoy.

Garlic Dill Leg Of Lamb

Servings: 2
Cooking Time: 21 Minutes
Ingredients:

- 9 oz leg of lamb, boneless
- 1 teaspoon minced garlic
- 2 tablespoons butter, softened
- ½ teaspoon dried dill
- ½ teaspoon salt

Directions:

1. In the shallow bowl mix up minced garlic, butter, dried dill, and salt. Then rub the leg of lamb with butter mixture and place it in the air fryer. Cook it at 380F for 21 minutes.

Creamy Burger & Potato Bake

Servings: 3
Cooking Time: 55 Minutes
Ingredients:

- salt to taste
- freshly ground pepper, to taste
- 1/2 (10.75 ounce) can condensed cream of mushroom soup
- 1/2-pound lean ground beef
- 1-1/2 cups peeled and thinly sliced potatoes
- 1/2 cup shredded Cheddar cheese
- 1/4 cup chopped onion
- 1/4 cup and 2 tablespoons milk

Directions:

1. Lightly grease baking pan of air fryer with cooking spray. Add ground beef. For 10 minutes, cook on 360F. Stir and crumble halfway through cooking time.
2. Meanwhile, in a bowl, whisk well pepper, salt, milk, onion, and mushroom soup. Mix well.
3. Drain fat off ground beef and transfer beef to a plate.
4. In same air fryer baking pan, layer ½ of potatoes on bottom, then ½ of soup mixture, and then ½ of beef. Repeat process.
5. Cover pan with foil.
6. Cook for 30 minutes. Remove foil and cook for another 15 minutes or until potatoes are tender.
7. Serve and enjoy.

Roasted Cilantro Lamb Chops

Servings: 6
Cooking Time: 24 Minutes
Ingredients:

- 12 lamb chops
- A pinch of salt and black pepper
- ½ cup cilantro, chopped
- 1 green chili pepper, chopped
- 1 garlic clove, minced

- Juice of 1 lime
- 3 tablespoons olive oil

Directions:

1. In a bowl, mix the lamb chops with the rest of the ingredients and rub well. Put the chops in your air fryer's basket and cook at 400 degrees F for 12 minutes on each side. Divide between plates and serve.

Tuscan Beef With Herb Vinegar

Servings: 3

Cooking Time: 20 Minutes

Ingredients:

- 3 sprigs fresh thyme, chopped
- 1/3 cup herb vinegar
- 2 teaspoons Tuscan seasoning
- 3 beef chops
- 2 teaspoons garlic powder
- Kosher salt and ground black pepper, to taste

Directions:

1. Toss the beef chops with the other ingredients.
2. Roast at 395 degrees F for 16 minutes, turning once or twice. Afterward, taste for doneness, add the seasonings and serve warm. Bon appétit!

Garlic Pork Medallions

Servings: 4

Cooking Time: 50 Minutes

Ingredients:

- 1-pound pork loin
- 2 tablespoons apple cider vinegar
- 2 tablespoons lemon juice
- ¼ cup heavy cream
- 1 teaspoon salt
- 1 teaspoon white pepper
- 1 garlic clove, diced
- 3 spring onions, diced
- 1 teaspoon lemon zest, grated
- 2 tablespoons avocado oil

Directions:

1. Make the marinade: in the mixing bowl mix up apple cider vinegar, lemon juice, heavy cream, salt, white pepper, diced garlic, onion, and lemon zest. Then add avocado oil and whisk the marinade carefully. Chop the pork loin roughly and put in the marinade. Coat the meat in the marinade carefully (use the spoon for this) and leave it for 20 minutes in the fridge. Meanwhile, preheat the air fryer to 365F. Put the marinated meat in the air fryer and cook it for 50 minutes. Stir the meat during cooking to avoid burning.

Garlic-cumin'n Orange Juice Marinated Steak

Servings: 4

Cooking Time: 60 Minutes

Ingredients:

- ¼ cup orange juice
- 1 teaspoon ground cumin
- 2 pounds skirt steak, trimmed from excess fat
- 2 tablespoons lime juice
- 2 tablespoons olive oil
- 4 cloves of garlic, minced
- Salt and pepper to taste

Directions:

1. Place all ingredients in a mixing bowl and allow to marinate in the fridge for at least 2 hours
2. Preheat the air fryer to 390F.
3. Place the grill pan accessory in the air fryer.
4. Grill for 15 minutes per batch and flip the beef every 8 minutes for even grilling.
5. Meanwhile, pour the marinade on a saucepan and allow to simmer for 10 minutes or until the sauce thickens.
6. Slice the beef and pour over the sauce.

Wrapped Pork

Servings: 2

Cooking Time: 16 Minutes

Ingredients:

- 8 oz pork tenderloin

- 4 bacon slices
- ½ teaspoon salt
- 1 teaspoon olive oil
- ½ teaspoon chili powder

Directions:

1. Sprinkle the pork tenderloin with salt and chili powder. Then wrap it in the bacon slices and sprinkle with olive oil. Secure the bacon with toothpicks if needed. After this, preheat the air fryer to 375F. Put the wrapped pork tenderloin in the air fryer and cook it for 7 minutes. After this, carefully flip the meat on another side and cook it for 9 minutes more. When the meat is cooked, remove the toothpicks from it (if the toothpicks were used) and slice the meat.

Italian Sausage & Tomato Egg Bake

Servings: 1
Cooking Time: 16 Minutes
Ingredients:

- ½ Italian sausage, sliced into ¼-inch thick
- 1 tablespoon olive oil
- 3 eggs
- 4 cherry tomatoes (in half)
- Chopped parsley
- Grano Padano cheese (or parmesan)
- Salt/Pepper

Directions:

1. Lightly grease baking pan of air fryer with cooking spray.
2. Add Italian sausage and cook for 5 minutes at 360F.
3. Add olive oil and cherry tomatoes. Cook for another 6 minutes.
4. Meanwhile, whisk well eggs, parsley, cheese, salt, and pepper in a bowl.
5. Remove basket and toss the mixture a bit. Pour eggs over mixture.
6. Cook for another 5 minutes.
7. Serve and enjoy.

Sriracha-hoisin Glazed Grilled Beef

Servings: 5
Cooking Time: 16 Minutes
Ingredients:

- 1-pound flank steak, sliced at an angle 1" x ¼" thick
- 1 tablespoon lime juice
- 1 chopped green onions
- 1-1/2 teaspoons honey
- 1/2 clove garlic, minced
- 1/2 teaspoon kosher salt
- 1/2 teaspoon peeled and grated fresh ginger root
- 1/2 teaspoon sesame oil (optional)
- 1/2 teaspoon chile-garlic sauce (such as Sriracha®)
- 1-1/2 teaspoons toasted sesame seeds
- 1/4 cup hoisin sauce
- 1/4 teaspoon crushed red pepper flakes
- 1/8 teaspoon ground black pepper

Directions:

1. In a shallow dish, mix well pepper, red pepper flakes, chile-garlic sauce, sesame oil, ginger, salt, honey, lime juice, and hoisin sauce. Add steak and toss well to coat. Marinate in the ref for 3 hours.
2. Thread steak in skewers. Place on skewer rack in air fryer.
3. For 8 minutes, cook on 360F. If needed, cook in batches.
4. Serve and enjoy with a drizzle of green onions and sesame seeds.

Orange Carne Asada

Servings: 4
Cooking Time: 14 Minutes
Ingredients:

- ¼ lime
- 2 tablespoons orange juice
- 1 teaspoon dried cilantro
- 1 chili pepper, chopped
- 1 tablespoon sesame oil

- 1 tablespoon apple cider vinegar
- ½ teaspoon chili paste
- ½ teaspoon ground cumin
- ½ teaspoon salt
- 1-pound beef skirt steak

Directions:

1. Chop the lime roughly and put it in the blender. Add orange juice, dried cilantro, chili pepper, sesame oil, apple cider vinegar, chili paste, ground cumin, and salt. Blend the mixture until smooth. Cut the skirt steak on 4 servings. Then brush every steak with blended lime mixture and leave for 10 minutes to marinate. Meanwhile, preheat the air fryer to 400F. Put the steaks in the air fryer in one layer and cook them for 7 minutes. Flip the meat on another side and cook it for 7 minutes more.

Sloppy Joes With A Twist

Servings: 4

Cooking Time: 45 Minutes

Ingredients:

- 1 tablespoon olive oil
- 1 shallot, chopped
- 2 garlic cloves, minced
- 1 bell pepper, chopped
- 1 pound ground pork
- 1 ripe medium-sized tomato, pureed
- 1 tablespoon poultry seasoning blend
- Dash ground allspice
- Keto Buns:
- 1/3 cup ricotta cheese, crumbled
- 2/3 cup part skim mozzarella cheese, shredded
- 1 egg
- 1/3 cup coconut flour
- 1/2 cup almond flour
- 1 teaspoon baking soda
- 1 ½ tablespoons plain whey protein isolate

Directions:

1. Start by preheating your Air Fryer to 390 degrees F. Heat the olive oil for a few minutes.

2. Once hot, sauté the shallots until just tender. Add the garlic and bell pepper; cook for 4 minutes more or until they are aromatic.

3. Add the ground pork and cook for 5 minutes more, crumbling with a fork. Next step, stir in the pureed tomatoes and spices. Decrease the temperature to 365 degrees F and cook another 10 minutes. Reserve.

4. To make the keto buns, microwave the cheese for 1 minute 30 seconds, stirring twice. Add the cheese to the bowl of a food processor and blend well. Fold in the egg and mix again.

5. Add in the flour, baking soda, and plain whey protein isolate; blend again. Scrape the batter onto the center of a lightly greased cling film.

6. Form the dough into a disk and transfer to your freezer to cool; cut into 4 pieces and transfer to a parchment-lined baking pan (make sure to grease your hands). Bake in the preheated oven at 400 degrees F for about 14 minutes.

7. Spoon the meat mixture into keto buns and transfer them to the cooking basket. Cook for 7 minutes or until thoroughly warmed.

Grandma's Meatballs With Spicy Sauce

Servings: 4

Cooking Time: 20 Minutes

Ingredients:

- 4 tablespoons pork rinds
- 1/3 cup green onion
- 1 pound beef sausage meat
- 3 garlic cloves, minced
- 1/3 teaspoon ground black pepper
- Sea salt, to taste
- For the sauce:
- 2 tablespoons Worcestershire sauce
- 1/3 yellow onion, minced
- Dash of Tabasco sauce
- 1/3 cup tomato paste
- 1 teaspoon cumin powder
- 1/2 tablespoon balsamic vinegar

Directions:

1. Knead all of the above ingredients until everything is well incorporated.
2. Roll into balls and cook in the preheated Air Fryer at 365 degrees for 13 minutes.
3. In the meantime, in a saucepan, cook the ingredients for the sauce until thoroughly warmed. Serve your meatballs with the tomato sauce and enjoy!

Lamb And Vinaigrette

Servings: 4
Cooking Time: 30 Minutes
Ingredients:

- 4 lamb loin slices
- A pinch of salt and black pepper
- 3 garlic cloves, minced
- 2 teaspoons thyme, chopped
- 2 tablespoons olive oil
- 1/3 cup parsley, chopped
- 1/3 cup sun-dried tomatoes, chopped
- 2 tablespoons balsamic vinegar
- 2 tablespoons water

Directions:

1. In a blender, combine all the ingredients except the lamb slices and pulse well. In a bowl, mix the lamb with the tomato vinaigrette and toss well. Put the lamb in your air fryer's basket and cook at 380 degrees F for 15 minutes on each side. Divide everything between plates and serve.

Betty's Beef Roast

Servings: 6
Cooking Time: 65 Minutes
Ingredients:

- 2 lb. beef
- 1 tbsp. olive oil
- 1 tsp. dried rosemary
- 1 tsp. dried thyme
- ½ tsp. black pepper
- ½ tsp. oregano

- ½ tsp. garlic powder
- 1 tsp. salt
- 1 tsp. onion powder

Directions:

1. Preheat the Air Fryer to 330°F.
2. In a small bowl, mix together all of the spices.
3. Coat the beef with a brushing of olive oil.
4. Massage the spice mixture into the beef.
5. Transfer the meat to the Air Fryer and cook for 30 minutes. Turn it over and cook on the other side for another 25 minutes.

Lamb Loin Chops With Garlic

Servings: 4
Cooking Time: 30 Minutes
Ingredients:

- 3 garlic cloves, crushed
- 1 tablespoon fresh lemon juice
- 1 teaspoon olive oil
- 1 tablespoon Za'atar*
- Kosher salt and ground black pepper, as required
- 8 (3½-ounces) bone-in lamb loin chops, trimmed

Directions:

1. In a large bowl, mix together the garlic, lemon juice, oil, Za'atar, salt, and black pepper.
2. Add chops and generously coat with the mixture.
3. Set the temperature of air fryer to 400 degrees F. Grease an air fryer basket.
4. Arrange chops into the prepared air fryer basket in a single layer in 2 batches.
5. Air Fry for about 15 minutes, flipping once after 4-5 minutes per side.
6. Remove from air fryer and transfer the chops onto plates.
7. Serve hot.

Flavorsome Pork Chops With Peanut Sauce

Servings: 4
Cooking Time: 12 Minutes
Ingredients:

- 1 pound pork chops, cubed into 1-inch size
- 1 shallot, chopped finely
- ¾ cup ground peanuts
- ¾ cup coconut milk
- For Pork:
- 1 teaspoon fresh ginger, minced
- 1 garlic clove, minced
- 2 tablespoon soy sauce
- 1 tablespoon olive oil
- 1 teaspoon hot pepper sauce
- For Peanut Sauce:
- 1 tablespoon olive oil
- 1 garlic clove, minced
- 1 teaspoon ground coriander
- 1 tablespoon olive oil
- 1 teaspoon hot pepper sauce

Directions:

1. Preheat the Air fryer to 390F and grease an Air fryer basket.
2. For Pork:
3. Mix all the ingredients in a bowl and keep aside for about 30 minutes.
4. Arrange the chops in the Air fryer basket and cook for about 12 minutes, flipping once in between.
5. For Peanut Sauce:
6. Heat olive oil in a pan on medium heat and add shallot and garlic.
7. Sauté for about 3 minutes and stir in coriander.
8. Sauté for about 1 minute and add rest of the ingredients.
9. Cook for about 5 minutes and pour over the pork chops to serve.

Ground Beef Mix

Servings: 4
Cooking Time: 20 Minutes

Ingredients:

- 1 pound beef, ground
- A pinch of salt and black pepper
- A drizzle of olive oil
- 2 spring onions, chopped
- 3 red chilies, chopped
- 1 cup beef stock
- 6 garlic cloves, minced
- 1 green bell pepper, chopped
- 8 ounces tomatoes, chopped
- 2 tablespoons chili powder

Directions:

1. Heat up a pan that fits your air fryer with the oil over medium-high heat, add the beef and brown for 3 minutes. Add the rest of the ingredients, toss, put the pan in the fryer and cook at 380 degrees F for 16 minutes. Divide into bowls and serve.

Must-serve Cajun Beef Tenderloin

Servings: 2
Cooking Time: 60 Minutes

Ingredients:

- 1/3 cup beef broth
- 2 tablespoons Cajun seasoning, crushed
- 1/2 teaspoon garlic powder
- 7 ounce beef tenderloins
- ½ tablespoon pear cider vinegar
- 1/3 teaspoon cayenne pepper
- 1 ½ tablespoon olive oil
- 1/2 teaspoon freshly ground black pepper
- 1 teaspoon salt

Directions:

1. Firstly, coat the beef tenderloins with salt, cayenne pepper, and black pepper.
2. Mix the remaining items in a medium-sized bowl; let the meat marinate for 40 minutes in this mixture.
3. Roast the beef for about 22 minutes at 385 degrees F, turning it halfway through the cooking time. Bon appétit!

Beef With Ghee Mushroom Mix

Servings: 4

Cooking Time: 25 Minutes

Ingredients:

- 4 beef steaks
- 1 tablespoon olive oil
- A pinch of salt and black pepper
- 2 tablespoons ghee, melted
- 2 garlic cloves, minced
- 5 cups wild mushrooms, sliced
- 1 tablespoon parsley, chopped

Directions:

1. Heat up a pan that fits the air fryer with the oil over medium-high heat, add the steaks and sear them for 2 minutes on each side. Add the rest of the ingredients, toss, transfer the pan to your air fryer and cook at 380 degrees F for 20 minutes. Divide between plates and serve.

Mustard Beef And Garlic Spinach

Servings: 4

Cooking Time: 20 Minutes

Ingredients:

- 3 garlic cloves, minced
- 1 and ½ pound beef, cut into strips
- 2 tablespoons coconut oil, melted
- 2 cups baby spinach
- 2 tablespoons chives, chopped
- 4 tablespoons mustard
- Salt and black pepper to the taste

Directions:

1. In a pan that fits the air fryer, combine all the ingredients, put the pan in the air fryer and cook at 390 degrees F for 20 minutes. Divide between plates and serve.

Tasty Stuffed Gyoza

Servings: 4

Cooking Time: 20 Minutes

Ingredients:

- ¼ cup chopped onion
- ¼ teaspoon ground cumin
- ¼ teaspoon paprika
- ½ cup chopped tomatoes
- 1 egg, beaten
- 1 tablespoon olive oil
- 1/8 teaspoon ground cinnamon
- 2 teaspoons chopped garlic
- 3 ounces chopped cremini mushrooms
- 3 ounces lean ground beef
- 6 pitted green olives, chopped
- 8 gyoza wrappers

Directions:

1. Heat oil in a skillet over medium flame and stir in the beef for 3 minutes. Add the onions and garlic until fragrant. Stir in the mushrooms, olives, paprika, cumin, cinnamon, and tomatoes.

2. Close the lid and allow to simmer for 5 minutes. Allow to cool before making the empanada.

3. Place the meat mixture in the middle of the gyoza wrapper. Fold the gyoza wrapper and seal the edges by brushing with the egg mixture.

4. Preheat the air fryer to 390F.

5. Place the grill pan accessory.

6. Place the prepared empanada on the grill pan accessory.

7. Cook for 10 minutes.

8. Flip the empanadas halfway through the cooking time.

Beef And Mushroom Meatloaf

Servings: 4

Cooking Time: 25 Minutes

Ingredients:

- 1 pound lean ground beef
- 1 small onion, finely chopped
- 3 tablespoons dry breadcrumbs
- 1 egg, lightly beaten
- 2 mushrooms, thickly sliced
- Salt and ground black pepper, as required
- 1 tablespoon olive oil

Directions:

1. Preheat the Air fryer to 390F and grease an Air fryer basket.
2. Mix the beef, onion, olive oil, breadcrumbs, egg, salt, and black pepper in a bowl until well combined.
3. Shape the mixture into loaves and top with mushroom slices.
4. Arrange the loaves in the Air fryer basket and cook for about 25 minutes.
5. Cut into desired size wedges and serve warm.

Ham Pinwheels

Servings: 4
Cooking Time: 11 Minutes
Ingredients:
- 1 puff pastry sheet
- 10 ham slices
- 1 cup Gruyere cheese, shredded plus more for sprinkling
- 4 teaspoons Dijon mustard

Directions:
1. Preheat the Air fryer to 375F and grease an Air fryer basket.
2. Place the puff pastry onto a smooth surface and spread evenly with the mustard.
3. Top with the ham and ¾ cup cheese and roll the puff pastry.
4. Wrap the roll in plastic wrap and freeze for about 30 minutes.
5. Remove from the freezer and slice into ½-inch rounds.
6. Arrange the pinwheels in the Air fryer basket and cook for about 8 minutes.
7. Top with remaining cheese and cook for 3 more minutes.
8. Dish out in a platter and serve warm.

Spicy And Saucy Pork Sirloin

Servings: 3
Cooking Time: 55 Minutes
Ingredients:
- 2 teaspoons peanut oil

- 1 ½ pounds pork sirloin
- Coarse sea salt and ground black pepper, to taste
- 1 tablespoon smoked paprika
- 1/4 cup prepared salsa sauce

Directions:
1. Start by preheating your Air Fryer to 360 degrees F.
2. Drizzle the oil all over the pork sirloin. Sprinkle with salt, black pepper, and paprika.
3. Cook for 50 minutes in the preheated Air Fryer.
4. Remove the roast from the Air Fryer and shred with two forks. Mix in the salsa sauce. Enjoy!

Coriander Lamb With Pesto 'n Mint Dip

Servings: 4
Cooking Time: 16 Minutes
Ingredients:
- 1 1/2 teaspoons coriander seeds, ground in spice mill or in mortar with pestle
- 1 large red bell pepper, cut into 1-inch squares
- 1 small red onion, cut into 1-inch squares
- 1 tablespoon extra-virgin olive oil plus additional for brushing
- 1 teaspoon coarse kosher salt
- 1-pound trimmed lamb meat, cut into 1 1/4-inch cubes
- 4 large garlic cloves, minced
- Mint-Pesto Dip Ingredients
- 1 cup (packed) fresh mint leaves
- 2 tablespoons pine nuts
- 2 tablespoons freshly grated Parmesan cheese
- 1 tablespoon fresh lemon juice
- 1 medium garlic clove, peeled
- 1/2 cup (packed) fresh cilantro leaves
- 1/2 teaspoon coarse kosher salt
- 1/2 cup (or more) extra-virgin olive oil

Directions:
1. In a blender, puree all dip Ingredients until smooth and creamy. Transfer to a bowl and set aside.
2. In a large bowl, mix well coriander, salt, garlic, and oil. Add lamb, toss well to coat. Marinate for at least an hour in the ref.

3. The thread lamb, bell pepper, and onion alternately in a skewer. Repeat until all Ingredients re used up. Place in skewer rack in air fryer.

4. For 8 minutes, cook on 390F. Halfway through cooking time, turnover.

5. Serve and enjoy with sauce on the side.

Chili Loin Medallions

Servings: 4

Cooking Time: 15 Minutes

Ingredients:

- 1-pound pork loin
- 4 oz bacon, sliced
- 1 teaspoon ground cumin
- 1 teaspoon coconut oil, melted
- ½ teaspoon salt
- ½ teaspoon chili flakes

Directions:

1. Slice the pork loin on the meat medallions and sprinkle them with ground cumin, salt, and chili flakes. Then wrap every meat medallion in the sliced bacon and sprinkle with coconut oil. Place the wrapped medallions in the air fryer basket in one layer and cook them for 10 minutes at 375F. Then carefully flip the meat medallions on another side and cook them for 5 minutes more.

Classic Rosemary Pork Meatloaf

Servings: 6

Cooking Time: 30 Minutes

Ingredients:

- Non-stick cooking spray
- 1 shallot, finely chopped
- 1 rib celery, finely chopped
- 2 gloves garlic, minced
- 1 tablespoon Worcestershire sauce
- 3/4 pound spicy ground pork sausage
- 1/4 pound ground turkey
- 2 sprigs rosemary, leaves only, crushed
- 1/4 cup minced fresh parsley
- 1 egg, lightly whisked
- 3 tablespoons fresh panko
- Salt and freshly ground pepper, to your liking
- 1/3 cup tomato ketchup

Directions:

1. Spritz a cast-iron skillet with a cooking spray. Then, sauté the shallots, celery and garlic until just tender and fragrant.

2. Now, add Worcestershire sauce and both kinds of meat to the sautéed mixture. Remove from the heat. Add the rosemary, parsley, egg, fresh panko, salt, and pepper; mix to combine well.

3. Transfer the mixture to the baking pan and shape into a loaf. Cover the prepared meatloaf with tomato ketchup.

4. Air-fry at 390 degrees F for 25 minutes or until thoroughly warmed.

FISH & SEAFOOD RECIPES

Tuna & Potato Cakes

Servings: 4

Cooking Time: 12 Minutes

Ingredients:

- ½ tablespoon olive oil
- 1 onion, chopped
- 1 tablespoon fresh ginger, grated
- 1 green chili, seeded and finely chopped
- 2 (6-ounces) cans tuna, drained
- 1 medium boiled potato, mashed
- 2 tablespoons celery, finely chopped
- Salt, as required
- 1 cup breadcrumbs
- 1 egg

Directions:

1. Heat the olive oil in a frying pan and sauté onions, ginger, and green chili for about 30 seconds.
2. Add the tuna and stir fry for about 2-3 minutes or until all the liquid is absorbed.
3. Remove from heat and transfer the tuna mixture onto a large bowl. Set aside to cool.
4. In the bowl of tuna mixture, mix well mashed potato, celery, and salt.
5. Make 4 equal-sized patties from the mixture.
6. In a shallow bowl, place the breadcrumbs.
7. In another bowl, beat the egg.
8. Coat each patty with breadcrumbs, then dip into egg and finally, again coat with the breadcrumbs.
9. Set the temperature of air fryer to 390 degrees F. Grease an air fryer basket.
10. Arrange tuna cakes into the prepared air fryer basket in a single layer.
11. Air fry for about 2-3 minutes.
12. Flip the side and air fry for about 4-5 minutes.
13. Remove from air fryer and transfer the tuna cakes onto serving plates.
14. Serve warm.

Salmon And Garlic Sauce

Servings: 4

Cooking Time: 15 Minutes

Ingredients:

- 3 tablespoons parsley, chopped
- 4 salmon fillets, boneless
- ¼ cup ghee, melted
- 2 garlic cloves, minced
- 4 shallots, chopped
- Salt and black pepper to the taste

Directions:

1. Heat up a pan that fits the air fryer with the ghee over medium-high heat, add the garlic, shallots, salt, pepper and the parsley, stir and cook for 5 minutes. Add the salmon fillets, toss gently, introduce the pan in the air fryer and cook at 380 degrees F for 15 minutes. Divide between plates and serve.

Snapper Fillets And Veggies Recipe

Servings: 2

Cooking Time: 24 Minutes

Ingredients:

- 2 red snapper fillets; boneless
- 1 tbsp. olive oil
- 1/2 cup red bell pepper; chopped.
- 1/2 cup green bell pepper; chopped
- 1/2 cup leeks; chopped.
- 1 tsp. tarragon; dried
- A splash of white wine
- Salt and black pepper to the taste

Directions:

1. In a heat proof dish that fits your air fryer; mix fish fillets with salt, pepper, oil, green bell pepper, red bell pepper, leeks, tarragon and wine; toss well everything, introduce in preheated air fryer at 350 °F and cook for 14 minutes; flipping fish fillets halfway. Divide fish and veggies on plates and serve warm.

Chipotle Salmon Fish Cakes

Servings: 4

Cooking Time: 2 Hours 15 Minutes

Ingredients:

- 1/2 teaspoon chipotle powder
- 1/2 teaspoon butter, at room temperature
- 1/3 teaspoon smoked cayenne pepper
- 1/2 teaspoon dried parsley flakes
- 1/3 teaspoon ground black pepper
- 1 pound salmon, chopped into 1/2 inch pieces
- 1 1/2 tablespoons milk
- 1/2 white onion, peeled and finely chopped
- 1 teaspoon fine sea salt
- 2 tablespoons coconut flour
- 2 tablespoons parmesan cheese, grated

Directions:

1. Place all ingredients in a large-sized mixing dish.
2. Shape into cakes and roll each cake over seasoned breadcrumbs. After that, refrigerate for about 2 hours.
3. Then, set your Air Fryer to cook at 395 degrees F for 13 minutes.
4. Serve warm with a dollop of sour cream if desired. Bon appétit!

Panko Fish Nuggets

Servings: 4

Cooking Time: 20 Minutes

Ingredients:

- Lemon juice to taste
- Salt and pepper to taste
- 1 tsp drilled dill
- 4 tbsp mayonnaise
- 1 whole egg, beaten
- 1 tbsp garlic powder
- 3 ½ oz breadcrumbs
- 1 tbsp paprika

Directions:

1. Preheat air fryer to 400 F. Season fish with salt and pepper. In a bowl, mix beaten egg, lemon juice, and mayonnaise. In a separate bowl, mix breadcrumbs, paprika, dill, and garlic powder. Dredge fillets in egg mixture and then the garlic-paprika mix; repeat until all fillets are prepared.

Place the fillets in your air fryer's cooking basket and cook for 15 minutes. Serve and enjoy!

Shrimp And Zucchini Mix

Servings: 4

Cooking Time: 8 Minutes

Ingredients:

- 2 red onions, cut into chunks
- 3 zucchinis, cut in medium chunks
- 1 pound shrimp, peeled and deveined
- 2 tablespoons olive oil
- ¼ cup tomato sauce
- Salt and black pepper to taste
- 1 garlic clove, minced
- 1 tablespoon lemon juice
- ½ cup parsley, chopped

Directions:

1. In a baking dish that fits your air fryer, mix all the ingredients except the parsley; toss well.
2. Place the baking dish into the fryer and cook at 400 degrees F for 8 minutes.
3. Add the parsley and stir.
4. Divide everything between plates and serve.

Asian Shrimp Medley

Servings: 4

Cooking Time: 20 Minutes

Ingredients:

- 2 whole onions, chopped
- 3 tbsp butter
- 1 ½ tbsp sugar
- 2 tbsp soy sauce
- 2 cloves garlic, chopped
- 2 tsp lime juice
- 1 tsp ginger, chopped

Directions:

1. Preheat your air fryer to 340 F, and in a bowl, mix lime juice, soy sauce, ginger, garlic, sugar and butter.

2. Add the mixture to a frying pan and warm over medium heat. Add in the chopped onions, and cook for 1 minute until translucent. Pour the mixture over shrimp, toss well and set aside for 30 minutes. Then, place the mixture in the air fryer's basket and cook for 8 minutes.

Crab Legs

Servings: 3
Cooking Time: 20 Minutes
Ingredients:
- 3 lb. crab legs
- ¼ cup salted butter, melted and divided
- ½ lemon, juiced
- ¼ tsp. garlic powder

Directions:
1. In a bowl, toss the crab legs and two tablespoons of the melted butter together. Place the crab legs in the basket of the fryer.
2. Cook at 400°F for fifteen minutes, giving the basket a good shake halfway through.
3. Combine the remaining butter with the lemon juice and garlic powder.
4. Crack open the cooked crab legs and remove the meat. Serve with the butter dip on the side and enjoy!

Oregano & Cumin Flavored Salmon Grill

Servings: 4
Cooking Time: 15 Minutes
Ingredients:
- 1 1/2 pounds skinless salmon fillet (preferably wild), cut into 1" pieces
- 1 teaspoon ground cumin
- 1 teaspoon kosher salt
- 1/4 teaspoon crushed red pepper flakes
- 2 lemons, very thinly sliced into rounds
- 2 tablespoons chopped fresh oregano
- 2 tablespoons olive oil
- 2 teaspoons sesame seeds

Directions:

1. In a small bowl, mix well oregano, sesame seeds, cumin, salt, and pepper flakes.
2. Thread salmon and folded lemon slices in a skewer. Brush with oil and sprinkle with spice.
3. Place skewers on air fryer skewer rack.
4. For 5 minutes, cook on 360F. If needed, cook in batches.
5. Serve and enjoy.

Fish Tacos

Servings: 4
Cooking Time: 15 Minutes
Ingredients:
- 1 halibut fillet
- 2 tbsp olive oil1
- ½ cup flour, divided
- 1 can of beer
- 1 tsp salt
- 4 tbsp peach salsa
- 4 tsp chopped cilantro
- 1 tsp baking powder

Directions:
1. Preheat the air fryer to 390 F, and combine 1 cup of flour, baking, powder and salt. Pour in some of the beer, enough to form a batter-like consistency. Save the rest of the beer to gulp with the taco.
2. Slice the fillet into 4 strips and toss them in half cup of flour. Dip them into the beer batter and arrange on a lined baking sheet. Cook in the air fryer for 8 minutes. Spread the peach salsa on the tortillas. Top each tortilla with one fish strip and chopped cilantro.

Salad Niçoise With Peppery Halibut

Servings: 6
Cooking Time: 15 Minutes
Ingredients:
- 1 ½ pounds halibut fillets
- 1 cup cherry tomatoes, halved
- 2 pounds mixed vegetables
- 2 tablespoons olive oil

- 4 cups torn lettuce leaves
- 4 large hard-boiled eggs, peeled and sliced
- Salt and pepper to taste

Directions:

1. Preheat the air fryer to 390F.
2. Place the grill pan accessory in the air fryer.
3. Rub the halibut with salt and pepper. Brush the fish with oil.
4. Place on the grill.
5. Surround the fish fillet with the mixed vegetables and cook for 15 minutes.
6. Assemble the salad by serving the fish fillet with grilled mixed vegetables, lettuce, cherry tomatoes, and hard-boiled eggs.

Garlic Parmesan Shrimp

Servings: 2
Cooking Time: 10 Minutes

Ingredients:

- 1 pound shrimp, deveined and peeled
- ½ cup parmesan cheese, grated
- ¼ cup cilantro, diced
- 1 tablespoon olive oil
- 1 teaspoon salt
- 1 teaspoon fresh cracked pepper
- 1 tablespoon lemon juice
- 6 garlic cloves, diced

Directions:

1. Preheat the Air fryer to 350F and grease an Air fryer basket.
2. Drizzle shrimp with olive oil and lemon juice and season with garlic, salt and cracked pepper.
3. Cover the bowl with plastic wrap and refrigerate for about 3 hours.
4. Stir in the parmesan cheese and cilantro to the bowl and transfer to the Air fryer basket.
5. Cook for about 10 minutes and serve immediately.

Italian Shrimp Scampi

Servings: 4

Cooking Time: 20 Minutes

Ingredients:

- 2 egg whites
- 1/2 cup coconut flour
- 1 cup Parmigiano-Reggiano, grated
- 1/2 teaspoon celery seeds
- 1/2 teaspoon porcini powder
- 1/2 teaspoon onion powder
- 1 teaspoon garlic powder
- 1/2 teaspoon dried rosemary
- 1/2 teaspoon sea salt
- 1/2 teaspoon ground black pepper
- 1 ½ pounds shrimp, deveined

Directions:

1. Whisk the egg with coconut flour and Parmigiano-Reggiano. Add in seasonings and mix to combine well.
2. Dip your shrimp in the batter. Roll until they are covered on all sides.
3. Cook in the preheated Air Fryer at 390 degrees F for 5 to 7 minutes or until golden brown. Work in batches. Serve with lemon wedges if desired.

Fried Anchovies

Servings: 4
Cooking Time: 6 Minutes

Ingredients:

- 1-pound anchovies
- ¼ cup coconut flour
- 2 eggs, beaten
- 1 teaspoon salt
- 1 teaspoon ground black pepper
- 1 tablespoon lemon juice
- 1 tablespoon sesame oil

Directions:

1. Trim and wash anchovies if needed and put in the big bowl. Add salt and ground black pepper. Mix up the anchovies. Then add eggs and stir the fish until you get a homogenous mixture. After this coat every anchovies fish in the coconut flour. Brush the air fryer pan with sesame oil. Place the anchovies in the pan in one layer. Preheat the air fryer to 400F.

Put the pan with anchovies in the air fryer and cook them for 6 minutes or until anchovies are golden brown.

Creamed Trout Salad

Servings: 2
Cooking Time: 20 Minutes
Ingredients:
- 1/2 pound trout fillets, skinless
- 2 tablespoons horseradish, prepared, drained
- 1/4 cup mayonnaise
- 1 tablespoon fresh lemon juice
- 1 teaspoon mustard
- Salt and ground white pepper, to taste
- 6 ounces chickpeas, canned and drained
- 1 red onion, thinly sliced
- 1 cup Iceberg lettuce, torn into pieces

Directions:
1. Spritz the Air Fryer basket with cooking spray.
2. Cook the trout fillets in the preheated Air Fryer at 395 degrees F for 10 minutes or until opaque. Make sure to turn them halfway through the cooking time.
3. Break the fish into bite-sized chunks and place in the refrigerator to cool. Toss your fish with the remaining ingredients. Bon appétit!

Aromatic Shrimp With Herbs

Servings: 4
Cooking Time: 40 Minutes
Ingredients:
- 1/2 tablespoon fresh basil leaves, chopped
- 1 ½ pounds shrimp, shelled and deveined
- 1 ½ tablespoons olive oil
- 3 cloves garlic, minced
- 1 teaspoon smoked cayenne pepper
- 1/2 teaspoon fresh mint, roughly chopped
- ½ teaspoon ginger, freshly grated
- 1 teaspoon sea salt

Directions:

1. Firstly, set your Air Fryer to cook at 395 degrees F.
2. In a mixing dish, combine all of the above items; toss until everything is well combined and let it stand for about 28 minutes.
3. Air-fry for 3 to 4 minutes. Bon appétit!

Lime Salmon

Servings: 6
Cooking Time: 12 Minutes
Ingredients:
- 2 salmon fillets, boneless
- 1 lime, sliced
- Juice of 1 lime
- ½ cup butter, melted
- ½ cup olive oil
- 3 garlic cloves, minced
- 2 shallots, chopped
- Salt and black pepper to taste
- 6 green onions, chopped

Directions:

1. In a bowl, mix the salmon with the lime juice, butter, oil, garlic, shallots, salt, pepper, and the green onions; rub well.
2. Transfer the fish to your air fryer, top with the lime slices, and cook at 380 degrees F for 6 minutes on each side.
3. Serve with a side salad.

Coconut Calamari

Servings: 2
Cooking Time: 6 Minutes
Ingredients:
- 6 oz calamari, trimmed
- 2 tablespoons coconut flakes
- 1 egg, beaten
- 1 teaspoon Italian seasonings
- Cooking spray

Directions:

1. Slice the calamari into the rings and sprinkle them with Italian seasonings. Then transfer the calamari rings in the bowl with a beaten egg and stir them gently. After this, sprinkle the calamari rings with coconut flakes and shake well. Preheat the air fryer to 400F. Put the calamari rings in the air fryer basket and spray them with cooking spray. Cook the meal for 3 minutes. Then gently stir the calamari and cook them for 3 minutes more.

Spicy Mackerel

Servings: 2
Cooking Time: 20 Minutes
Ingredients:
- 2 mackerel fillets
- 2 tbsp. red chili flakes
- 2 tsp. garlic, minced
- 1 tsp. lemon juice

Directions:
1. Season the mackerel fillets with the red pepper flakes, minced garlic, and a drizzle of lemon juice. Allow to sit for five minutes.
2. Preheat your fryer at 350°F.
3. Cook the mackerel for five minutes, before opening the drawer, flipping the fillets, and allowing to cook on the other side for another five minutes.
4. Plate the fillets, making sure to spoon any remaining juice over them before serving.

Foil Packet Salmon

Servings: 2
Cooking Time: 15 Minutes
Ingredients:
- 2 x 4-oz. skinless salmon fillets
- 2 tbsp. unsalted butter, melted
- ½ tsp. garlic powder
- 1 medium lemon
- ½ tsp. dried dill

Directions:
1. Take a sheet of aluminum foil and cut into two squares measuring roughly 5" x 5". Lay each of the

salmon fillets at the center of each piece. Brush both fillets with a tablespoon of bullet and season with a quarter-teaspoon of garlic powder.
2. Halve the lemon and grate the skin of one half over the fish. Cut four half-slices of lemon, using two to top each fillet. Season each fillet with a quarter-teaspoon of dill.
3. Fold the tops and sides of the aluminum foil over the fish to create a kind of packet. Place each one in the fryer.
4. Cook for twelve minutes at 400°F.
5. The salmon is ready when it flakes easily. Serve hot.

Shrimp Skewers

Servings: 5
Cooking Time: 5 Minutes
Ingredients:
- 4-pounds shrimps, peeled
- 2 tablespoons fresh cilantro, chopped
- 2 tablespoons apple cider vinegar
- 1 teaspoon ground coriander
- 1 tablespoon avocado oil
- Cooking spray

Directions:
1. In the shallow bowl mix up avocado oil, ground coriander, apple cider vinegar, and fresh cilantro. Then put the shrimps in the big bowl and sprinkle with avocado oil mixture. Mix them well and leave for 10 minutes to marinate. After this, string the shrimps on the skewers. Preheat the air fryer to 400F. Arrange the shrimp skewers in the air fryer and cook them for 5 minutes.

Shrimp Magic

Servings: 3
Cooking Time: 5 Minutes
Ingredients:
- 1½ pounds shrimps, peeled and deveined
- Lemongrass stalks
- 4 garlic cloves, minced

- 1 red chili pepper, seeded and chopped
- 2 tablespoons olive oil
- ½ teaspoon smoked paprika

Directions:

1. Preheat the Air fryer to 390F and grease an Air fryer basket.
2. Mix all the ingredients in a large bowl and refrigerate to marinate for about 2 hours.
3. Thread the shrimps onto lemongrass stalks and transfer into the Air fryer basket.
4. Cook for about 5 minutes and dish out to serve warm.

Coriander Cod And Green Beans

Servings: 4
Cooking Time: 15 Minutes
Ingredients:

- 12 oz cod fillet
- ½ cup green beans, trimmed and halved
- 1 tablespoon avocado oil
- 1 teaspoon salt
- 1 teaspoon ground coriander

Directions:

1. Cut the cod fillet on 4 servings and sprinkle every serving with salt and ground coriander. After this, place the fish on 4 foil squares. Top them with green beans and avocado oil and wrap them into parcels. Preheat the air fryer to 400F. Place the cod parcels in the air fryer and cook them for 15 minutes.

Whitefish Cakes

Servings: 4
Cooking Time: 1 Hr. 20 Minutes
Ingredients:

- 1 ½ cups whitefish fillets, minced
- 1 ½ cups green beans, finely chopped
- ½ cup scallions, chopped
- 1 chili pepper, deveined and minced
- 1 tbsp. red curry paste
- 1 tsp. sugar

- 1 tbsp. fish sauce
- 2 tbsp. apple cider vinegar
- 1 tsp. water
- Sea salt flakes, to taste
- ½ tsp. cracked black peppercorns
- 1 ½ teaspoons butter, at room temperature
- 1 lemon

Directions:

1. Place all of the ingredients a bowl, following the order in which they are listed.
2. Combine well with a spatula or your hands.
3. Mold the mixture into several small cakes and refrigerate for 1 hour.
4. Put a piece of aluminum foil in the cooking basket and lay the cakes on top.
5. Cook at 390°F for 10 minutes. Turn each fish cake over before air-frying for another 5 minutes.
6. Serve the fish cakes with a side of cucumber relish.

Fried Tilapia Bites

Servings: 4
Cooking Time: 20 Minutes
Ingredients:

- ½ cup cornflakes
- 3 tbsp flour
- 1 egg, beaten
- Salt to taste
- Lemon wedges for serving

Directions:

1. Preheat your Air Fryer to 390 F. Spray the air fryer basket with cooking spray.
2. Put the flour, egg, and conflakes each into a different bowl, three bowls in total. Add salt egg bowl and mix well. Dip the tilapia first in the flour, then in the egg, and lastly, coat in the cornflakes. Lay on the air fryer basket. Spray with cooking spray and cook for 5 minutes. Slide out the fryer basket and shake the shrimp; cook further for 5 minutes. Serve with lemon wedges.

Homemade Cod Fillets

Servings: 4
Cooking Time: 15 Minutes
Ingredients:

- 4 cod fillets
- ¼ tsp. fine sea salt
- ¼ tsp. ground black pepper, or more to taste
- 1 tsp. cayenne pepper
- ½ cup non-dairy milk
- ½ cup fresh Italian parsley, coarsely chopped
- 1 tsp. dried basil
- ½ tsp. dried oregano
- 1 Italian pepper, chopped
- 4 garlic cloves, minced

Directions:

1. Lightly grease a baking dish with some vegetable oil.
2. Coat the cod fillets with salt, pepper, and cayenne pepper.
3. Blend the rest of the ingredients in a food processor. Cover the fish fillets in this mixture.
4. Transfer the fillets to the Air Fryer and cook at 380°F for 10 to 12 minutes, ensure the cod is flaky before serving.

Catfish With Spring Onions And Avocado

Servings: 4
Cooking Time: 15 Minutes
Ingredients:

- 2 teaspoons oregano, dried
- 2 teaspoons cumin, ground
- 2 teaspoons sweet paprika
- A pinch of salt and black pepper
- 4 catfish fillets
- 1 avocado, peeled and cubed
- ½ cup spring onions, chopped
- 2 tablespoons cilantro, chopped
- 2 teaspoons olive oil
- 2 tablespoons lemon juice

Directions:

1. In a bowl, mix all the ingredients except the fish and toss. Arrange this in a baking pan that fits the air fryer, top with the fish, introduce the pan in the machine and cook at 360 degrees F for 15 minutes, flipping the fish halfway. Divide between plates and serve.

Nutritious Salmon And Veggie Patties

Servings: 6
Cooking Time: 7 Minutes
Ingredients:

- 3 large russet potatoes, boiled and mashed
- 1 (6-ounce) salmon fillet
- 1 egg
- ¾ cup frozen vegetables, parboiled and drained
- 1 cup breadcrumbs
- 2 tablespoons dried parsley, chopped
- 1 teaspoon dried dill, chopped
- Salt and freshly ground pepper, to taste
- ¼ cup olive oil

Directions:

1. Preheat the Air fryer to 355F and line a pan with foil paper.
2. Place salmon in the Air fryer basket and cook for about 5 minutes.
3. Dish out the salmon in a large bowl and flake with a fork.
4. Mix potatoes, egg, parboiled vegetables, parsley, dill, salt and black pepper until well combined.
5. Make 6 equal sized patties from the mixture and coat the patties evenly with breadcrumbs.
6. Drizzle with the olive oil and arrange the patties in the pan.
7. Transfer into the Air fryer basket and cook for about 12 minutes, flipping once in between.

Dilled Crab And Cauliflower Cakes

Servings: 4
Cooking Time: 20 Minutes
Ingredients:

- 1 ½ tablespoons mayonnaise

- 1/2 teaspoon whole-grain mustard
- 2 eggs, well beaten
- 1/3 teaspoon ground black pepper
- 1/2 pound cup mashed cauliflower
- 1/2 teaspoon dried dill weed
- 1/2 pound crabmeat
- A pinch of salt
- 1 ½ tablespoons softened butter

Directions:

1. Mix all the ingredients thoroughly. Shape into 4 patties.
2. Then, spritz your patties with cooking oil.
3. Air-fry at 365 degrees F for 12 minutes, turning halfway through. Serve over boiled potatoes. Bon appétit!

Pistachio Crusted Salmon

Servings: 1
Cooking Time: 15 Minutes
Ingredients:

- 1 tsp mustard
- 3 tbsp pistachios
- A pinch of sea salt
- A pinch of garlic powder
- A pinch of black pepper
- 1 tsp lemon juice
- 1 tsp grated Parmesan cheese
- 1 tsp olive oil

Directions:

1. Preheat the air fryer to 350 F, and whisk mustard and lemon juice together. Season the salmon with salt, pepper, and garlic powder. Brush the olive oil on all sides. Brush the mustard mixture onto salmon.
2. Chop the pistachios finely and combine them with the Parmesan cheese; sprinkle on top of the salmon. Place the salmon in the air fryer basket with the skin side down. Cook for 12 minutes, or to your liking.

Mahi Mahi With Green Beans

Servings: 4
Cooking Time: 12 Minutes
Ingredients:

- 5 cups green beans
- 2 tablespoons fresh dill, chopped
- 4 (6-ounces) Mahi Mahi fillets
- 1 tablespoon avocado oil
- Salt, as required
- 2 garlic cloves, minced
- 2 tablespoons fresh lemon juice
- 1 tablespoon olive oil

Directions:

1. Preheat the Air fryer to 375F and grease an Air fryer basket.
2. Mix the green beans, avocado oil and salt in a large bowl.
3. Arrange green beans into the Air fryer basket and cook for about 6 minutes.
4. Combine garlic, dill, lemon juice, salt and olive oil in a bowl.
5. Coat Mahi Mahi in this garlic mixture and place on the top of green beans.
6. Cook for 6 more minutes and dish out to serve warm.

Rich Crab Croquettes

Servings: 4
Cooking Time: 30 Minutes
Ingredients:

- 1 ½ lb lump crab meat
- 3 egg whites, beaten
- ⅓ cup sour cream
- ⅓ cup mayonnaise
- 1 ½ tbsp olive oil
- 1 red pepper, chopped finely
- ⅓ cup chopped red onion
- 2 ½ tbsp chopped celery
- ½ tsp chopped tarragon
- ½ tsp chopped chives
- 1 tsp chopped parsley

- 1 tsp cayenne pepper
- Breading:
- 1 ½ cup breadcrumbs
- 2 tsp olive oil
- 1 cup flour
- 4 eggs, beaten
- Salt to taste

Directions:

1. Place a skillet over medium heat on a stovetop, add 1 ½ tbsp olive oil, red pepper, onion, and celery. Sauté for 5 minutes or until sweaty and translucent. Turn off heat. Add the breadcrumbs, the remaining olive oil, and salt to a food processor. Blend to mix evenly; set aside. In 2 separate bowls, add the flour and 4 eggs respectively, set aside.

2. In a separate bowl, add crabmeat, mayo, egg whites, sour cream, tarragon, chives, parsley, cayenne pepper, and celery sauté and mix evenly. Form bite-sized balls from the mixture and place onto a plate.

3. Preheat the air fryer to 390 F. Dip each crab meatball (croquettes) in the egg mixture and press them in the breadcrumb mixture. Place the croquettes in the fryer basket, avoid overcrowding. Close the air fryer and cook for 10 minutes or until golden brown. Remove them and plate them. Serve the crab croquettes with tomato dipping sauce and a side of vegetable fries.

Garlic-cilantro Over Salmon Steak

Servings: 2
Cooking Time: 15 Minutes
Ingredients:

- ½ cup Greek yogurt
- 1 cup cilantro leaves
- 1 teaspoon honey
- 2 cloves of garlic, minced
- 2 salmon steaks
- 2 tablespoons vegetable oil
- Salt and pepper to taste

Directions:

1. Preheat the air fryer to 390F.

2. Place the grill pan accessory in the air fryer.

3. Season the salmon steaks with salt and pepper. Brush with oil.

4. Grill for 15 minutes and make sure to flip halfway through the cooking time.

5. In a food processor, mix the garlic, cilantro leaves, yogurt and honey. Season with salt and pepper to taste. Pulse until smooth.

6. Serve the salmon steaks with the cilantro sauce.

Salmon With Cilantro And Citrus Sauce

Servings: 4
Cooking Time: 50 Minutes
Ingredients:

- 1 ½ pounds salmon steak
- ½ teaspoon grated lemon zest
- Freshly cracked mixed peppercorns, to taste
- 1/3 cup lemon juice
- Fresh chopped chives, for garnish
- 1/2 cup dry white wine
- 1/2 teaspoon fresh cilantro, chopped
- Fine sea salt, to taste

Directions:

1. To prepare the marinade, place all ingredients, except for salmon steak and chives, in a deep pan. Bring to a boil over medium-high flame until it has reduced by half. Allow it to cool down.

2. After that, allow salmon steak to marinate in the refrigerator approximately 40 minutes. Discard the marinade and transfer the fish steak to the preheated Air Fryer.

3. Air-fry at 400 degrees F for 9 to10 minutes. To finish, brush hot fish steaks with the reserved marinade, garnish with fresh chopped chives, and serve right away!

Lemon Tuna 'n Buttered Rice Puff

Servings: 6
Cooking Time: 60 Minutes
Ingredients:

- 1 teaspoon salt

56

- 2 egg yolks1 (12 ounce) can tuna, undrained
- 2 tablespoons grated onion
- 1 tablespoon lemon juice
- 2 egg whites
- 1 1/2 cups milk
- 1 1/3 cups water
- 1/3 cup butter
- 1/4 cup all-purpose flour
- 1/4 teaspoon ground black pepper
- 2/3 cup uncooked white rice

Directions:

1. In a saucepan bring water to a boil. Stir in rice, cover and cook on low fire until liquid is fully absorbed, around 20 minutes.
2. In another saucepan over medium fire, melt butter. Stir in pepper, salt, and flour. Cook for 2 minutes. Whisking constantly, slowly add milk. Continue cooking and stirring until thickened.
3. In medium bowl, whisk egg yolks. Slowly whisk in half of the thickened milk mixture. Add to pan of remaining milk and continue cooking and stirring for 2 more minutes. Stir in lemon juice, onion, tuna, and rice.
4. Lightly grease baking pan of air fryer with cooking spray. And transfer rice mixture.
5. Beat egg whites until stiff peak forms. Slowly fold into rice mixture.
6. Cover pan with foil.
7. For 20 minutes, cook on 360F.
8. Cook for 15 minutes at 390F until tops are lightly browned and the middle has set.
9. Serve and enjoy.

Louisiana-style Shrimp

Servings: 4
Cooking Time: 18 Minutes
Ingredients:

- 1 egg, beaten
- ¼ cup flour
- ¼ cup white breadcrumbs
- 2 tbsp Cajun seasoning
- Salt and black pepper to taste

- 1 lemon, cut into wedges

Directions:

1. Preheat your Air Fryer to 390 F. Spray the air fryer basket with cooking spray.
2. Beat the eggs in a bowl and season with salt and black pepper. In a separate bowl, mix white breadcrumbs with Cajun seasoning. In a third bowl, pour the flour.
3. Dip the shrimp in the flour and then in the eggs, and finally in the breadcrumb mixture. Spray with cooking spray and place in the cooking basket. Cook for 6 minutes, Slide out the fryer basket and flip; cook for 6 more minutes. Serve with lemon wedges.

Salmon With Asparagus

Servings: 2
Cooking Time: 11 Minutes
Ingredients:

- 2 (6-ounces) boneless salmon fillets
- 1½ tablespoons fresh lemon juice
- 1 tablespoon olive oil
- 2 tablespoons fresh parsley, roughly chopped
- 2 tablespoons fresh dill, roughly chopped
- 1 bunch asparagus
- Salt and ground black pepper, as required

Directions:

1. In a small bowl, mix well the lemon juice, oil, herbs, salt, and black pepper.
2. In another large bowl, mix together the salmon and ¾ of oil mixture.
3. In a second large bowl, add the asparagus and remaining oil mixture. Mix them well.
4. Set the temperature of air fryer to 400 degrees F. Grease an air fryer basket.
5. Arrange asparagus into the prepared air fryer basket.
6. Air fry for about 2-3 minutes.
7. Now, place the salmon fillets on top of asparagus and air fry for about 8 minutes.
8. Remove from air fryer and place the salmon fillets onto serving plates.
9. Serve hot alongside the asparagus.

Tasty Sockeye Fish

Servings: 2

Cooking Time: 25 Minutes

Ingredients:

- ½ bulb fennel, thinly sliced
- 4 tbsp melted butter
- Salt and pepper to taste
- 1-2 tsp fresh dill
- 2 sockeye salmon fillets
- 8 cherry tomatoes, halved
- ¼ cup fish stock

Directions:

1. Preheat air fryer to 400 F. Bring to a boil salted water over medium heat. Add the potatoes and blanch for 2 minutes; drain. Cut 2 large-sized rectangles of parchment paper of 13x15 inch size.

2. In a large bowl, mix potatoes, fennel, pepper, and salt. Divide the mixture between parchment paper pieces and sprinkle with dill. Top with fillets. Add cherry tomatoes on top and drizzle with butter; pour fish stock on top. Fold the squares and seal them. Cook the packets in the air fryer for 10 minutes.

Jamaican-jerk Seasoned Salmon

Servings: 2

Cooking Time: 12 Minutes

Ingredients:

- 1 ½ tablespoons mayonnaise
- 1 teaspoon grated lime zest
- 1/4 cup sour cream
- 1/4 cup sweetened shredded coconut, toasted
- 2 salmon fillets (6 ounces each)
- 2 teaspoons Caribbean jerk seasoning
- 4 tbsp cream of coconut
- 4 tbsp cup lime juice

Directions:

1. Lightly grease baking pan of air fryer with cooking spray. Add salmon with skin side down. Spread mayo on top and season with Caribbean jerk.

2. For 12 minutes, cook on 330F.

3. On medium low fire, place a pan and bring lime juice, lime zest, cream of coconut, and sour cream to a simmer. Mix well. Transfer to a bowl for dipping.

4. Serve and enjoy.

Frozen Sesame Fish Fillets

Servings: 5

Cooking Time: 20 Minutes

Ingredients:

- 5 biscuits, crumbled
- 3 tbsp flour
- 1 egg, beaten
- A pinch of salt
- A pinch of black pepper
- ¼ tsp rosemary
- 3 tbsp olive oil divided
- A handful of sesame seeds

Directions:

1. Preheat the air fryer to 390 F. Combine the flour, pepper and salt, in a shallow bowl. In another shallow bowl, combine the sesame seeds, crumbled biscuits, oil, and rosemary. Dip the fish fillets into the flour mixture first, then into the beaten egg, and finally, coat them with the sesame mixture.

2. Arrange them in the air fryer on a sheet of aluminum foil; cook the fish for 8 minutes. Flip the fillets over and cook for an additional 4 minutes. Serve and enjoy.

Lobster-spinach Lasagna Recipe From Maine

Servings: 6

Cooking Time: 50 Minutes

Ingredients:

- 1 (16 ounce) jar Alfredo pasta sauce
- 1 cup shredded Cheddar cheese
- 1 egg
- 1 pound cooked and cubed lobster meat
- 1 tablespoon chopped fresh parsley

- 1/2 (15 ounce) container ricotta cheese
- 1/2 cup grated Parmesan cheese
- 1/2 cup shredded mozzarella cheese
- 1/2 medium onion, minced
- 1/2 teaspoon freshly ground black pepper
- 1-1/2 teaspoons minced garlic
- 5-ounce package baby spinach leaves
- 8 no-boil lasagna noodles

Directions:

1. Mix well half of Parmesan, half of mozzarella, half of cheddar, egg, and ricotta cheese in a medium bowl. Stir in pepper, parsley, garlic, and onion.

2. Lightly grease baking pan of air fryer with cooking spray.

3. On bottom of pan, spread ½ of the Alfredo sauce, top with a single layer of lasagna noodles. Followed by 1/3 of lobster meat, 1/3 of ricotta cheese mixture, 1/3 of spinach. Repeat layering process until all ingredients are used up.

4. Sprinkle remaining cheese on top. Shake pan to settle lasagna and burst bubbles. Cover pan with foil.

5. For 30 minutes, cook on 360F.

6. Remove foil and cook for 10 minutes at 390F until tops are lightly browned.

7. Let it stand for 10 minutes.

8. Serve and enjoy.

Crispy Spicy-lime Fish Filet

Servings: 4
Cooking Time: 15 Minutes
Ingredients:

- 1 egg white, beaten
- 1 tablespoon lime juice, freshly squeezed
- 1 teaspoon lime zest
- 2 fish fillets, cut into pieces
- 2 tablespoon olive oil
- 5 tablespoons almond flour
- A dash of chili powder
- Salt and pepper to taste

Directions:

1. Preheat the air fryer.

2. Place all ingredients in a Ziploc bag and shake until all ingredients are well combined.

3. Place in the air fryer basket.

4. Cook for 15 minutes at 400F.

Fishman Cakes

Servings: 4
Cooking Time: 35 Minutes
Ingredients:

- 2 cups white fish
- 1 cup potatoes, mashed
- 1 tsp. mix herbs
- 1 tsp. mix spice
- 1 tsp. coriander
- 1 tsp. Worcestershire sauce
- 2 tsp. chili powder
- 1 tsp. milk
- 1 tsp. butter
- 1 small onion, diced
- ¼ cup bread crumbs
- Pepper and salt to taste

Directions:

1. Place all of the ingredients in a bowl and combine.

2. Using your hands, mold equal portions of the mixture into small patties and refrigerate for 2 hours.

3. Put the fish cakes in the Air Fryer basket and cook at 400°F for 15 minutes. Serve hot.

Citrusy Branzini On The Grill

Servings: 2
Cooking Time: 15 Minutes
Ingredients:

- 2 branzini fillets
- Salt and pepper to taste
- 3 lemons, juice freshly squeezed
- 2 oranges, juice freshly squeezed

Directions:

1. Place all ingredients in a Ziploc bag. Allow to marinate in the fridge for 2 hours.

2. Preheat the air fryer at 390F.

3. Place the grill pan accessory in the air fryer.

4. Place the fish on the grill pan and cook for 15 minutes until the fish is flaky.

Cocktail Prawns In Air Fryer

Servings: 1

Cooking Time: 8 Minutes

Ingredients:

- ½ teaspoon black pepper
- ½ teaspoon sea salt
- 1 tablespoon ketchup
- 1 tablespoon white wine vinegar
- 1 teaspoon chili flakes
- 1 teaspoon chili powder
- 12 prawns, shelled and deveined

Directions:

1. Preheat the air fryer to 390F.

2. Place the shrimps in a bowl.

3. Stir in the rest of the Ingredients until the shrimps are coated with the sauce.

4. Place the shrimps on the double layer rack and cook for 8 minutes.

5. Serve with mayonnaise if desired.

Chinese Garlic Shrimp

Servings: 5

Cooking Time: 15 Minutes

Ingredients:

- Juice of 1 lemon
- 1 tsp sugar
- 3 tbsp peanut oil
- 2 tbsp cornstarch
- 2 scallions, chopped
- ¼ tsp Chinese powder
- Chopped chili to taste
- Salt and black pepper to taste
- 4 garlic cloves

Directions:

1. Preheat air fryer to 370 F. In a Ziploc bag, mix lemon juice, sugar, pepper, half of oil, cornstarch, powder, Chinese powder and salt. Add in the shrimp and massage to coat evenly. Let sit for 10 minutes.

2. Add the remaining peanut oil, garlic, scallions, and chili to a pan, and fry for 5 minutes over medium heat. Place the marinated shrimp in your air fryer's basket and cover with the sauce. Cook for 10 minutes, until nice and crispy. Serve.

Lemony-sage On Grilled Swordfish

Servings: 2

Cooking Time: 16 Minutes

Ingredients:

- ½ lemon, sliced thinly in rounds
- 1 tbsp lemon juice
- 1 tsp parsley
- 1 zucchini, peeled and then thinly sliced in lengths
- 1/2-pound swordfish, sliced into 2-inch chunks
- 2 tbsp olive oil
- 6-8 sage leaves
- salt and pepper to taste

Directions:

1. In a shallow dish, mix well lemon juice, parsley, and sliced swordfish. Toss well to coat and generously season with pepper and salt. Marinate for at least 10 minutes.

2. Place one length of zucchini on a flat surface. Add one piece of fish and sage leaf. Roll zucchini and then thread into a skewer. Repeat process to remaining Ingredients.

3. Brush with oil and place on skewer rack in air fryer.

4. For 8 minutes, cook on 390F. If needed, cook in batches.

5. Serve and enjoy with lemon slices.

Squid Mix

Servings: 4

Cooking Time: 17 Minutes

Ingredients:

- 17 ounces squids, cleaned and cut into medium pieces
- ½ cup veggie stock
- 1½ tablespoons red chili powder
- Salt and black pepper to taste
- ¼ teaspoon turmeric powder
- 4 garlic cloves, minced
- ½ teaspoon cumin seeds
- 3 tablespoons olive oil
- ¼ teaspoon mustard seeds
- 1-inch ginger, minced

Directions:

1. Place all ingredients in a pan that fits your air fryer and mix well.
2. Insert the pan into the fryer and cook at 380 degrees F for 17 minutes.
3. Divide between plates and serve.

Japanese Ponzu Marinated Tuna

Servings: 4
Cooking Time: 10 Minutes
Ingredients:

- 1 cup Japanese ponzu sauce
- 2 tbsp sesame oil
- 1 tbsp red pepper flakes
- 2 tbsp ginger paste
- ¼ cup scallions, sliced
- Salt and black pepper to taste

Directions:

1. In a bowl, mix the ponzu sauce, sesame oil, red pepper flakes, ginger paste, salt, and black pepper. Add in the tuna and toss to coat. Cover and leave to marinate for 60 minutes in the fridge.
2. Preheat air Fryer to 380 F. Spray air fryer basket with cooking spray. Remove tuna from the fridge and arrange on the air fryer basket. Cook for 6 minutes, turning once. Top with scallions to serve.

Lemon And Oregano Tilapia Mix

Servings: 4
Cooking Time: 20 Minutes

Ingredients:

- 4 tilapia fillets, boneless and halved
- Salt and black pepper to the taste
- 1 cup roasted peppers, chopped
- ¼ cup keto tomato sauce
- 1 cup tomatoes, cubed
- 1 tablespoon lemon juice
- 2 tablespoons olive oil
- 1 teaspoon garlic powder
- 1 teaspoon oregano, dried

Directions:

1. In a baking dish that fits your air fryer, mix the fish with all the other ingredients, toss, introduce in your air fryer and cook at 380 degrees F for 20 minutes. Divide into bowls and serve.

Easy Prawns Alla Parmigiana

Servings: 4
Cooking Time: 20 Minutes
Ingredients:

- 2 egg whites
- 1 cup all-purpose flour
- 1 cup Parmigiano-Reggiano, grated
- 1/2 cup fine breadcrumbs
- 1/2 teaspoon celery seeds
- 1/2 teaspoon porcini powder
- 1/2 teaspoon onion powder
- 1 teaspoon garlic powder
- 1/2 teaspoon dried rosemary
- 1/2 teaspoon sea salt
- 1/2 teaspoon ground black pepper
- 1 ½ pounds prawns, deveined

Directions:

1. To make a breading station, whisk the egg whites in a shallow dish. In a separate dish, place the all-purpose flour.
2. In a third dish, thoroughly combine the Parmigiano-Reggiano, breadcrumbs, and seasonings; mix to combine well.
3. Dip the prawns in the flour, then, into the egg whites; lastly, dip them in the parm/breadcrumb mixture. Roll until they are covered on all sides.

4. Cook in the preheated Air Fryer at 390 degrees F for 5 to 7 minutes or until golden brown. Work in batches. Serve with lemon wedges if desired.

Cod Cakes

Servings: 6
Cooking Time: 14 Minutes
Ingredients:
- 1 pound cod fillet
- 1 teaspoon fresh lime zest, finely grated
- 1 egg
- 1 teaspoon red chili paste
- Salt, as required
- 1 tablespoon fresh lime juice
- 1/3 cup coconut, grated and divided
- 1 scallion, finely chopped
- 2 tablespoons fresh parsley, chopped

Directions:
1. For cod cakes: in a food processor, add the cod fillet, lime zest, egg, chili paste, salt, and lime juice and pulse until smooth.
2. Transfer the cod mixture into a bowl.
3. Add 2 tablespoons of coconut, scallion, and parsley. Mix until well combined.
4. Make 12 equal-sized round cakes from the mixture.
5. In a shallow bowl, place the remaining coconut.
6. Coat the cod cakes evenly with coconut.
7. Set the temperature of air fryer to 375 degrees F. Grease an air fryer basket.
8. Arrange cod cakes into the prepared air fryer basket in 2 batches in a single layer.
9. Air fry for about 7 minutes.
10. Remove from air fryer and place 2 cod cakes onto each serving plate.
11. Serve warm.

Cajun Fish Cakes With Cheese

Servings: 4
Cooking Time: 30 Minutes
Ingredients:
- 2 catfish fillets
- 1 cup all-purpose flour

- 3 ounces butter
- 1 teaspoon baking powder
- 1 teaspoon baking soda
- 1/2 cup buttermilk
- 1 teaspoon Cajun seasoning
- 1 cup Swiss cheese, shredded

Directions:
1. Bring a pot of salted water to a boil. Boil the fish fillets for 5 minutes or until it is opaque. Flake the fish into small pieces.
2. Mix the remaining ingredients in a bowl; add the fish and mix until well combined. Shape the fish mixture into 12 patties.
3. Cook in the preheated Air Fryer at 380 degrees F for 15 minutes. Work in batches. Enjoy!

Shrimp With Garlic And Goat Cheese

Servings: 2
Cooking Time: 10 Minutes
Ingredients:
- 1/2 tablespoon fresh parsley, roughly chopped
- 1 ½ tablespoons balsamic vinegar
- Sea salt flakes, to taste
- 1 pound shrimp, deveined
- 1 tablespoon coconut aminos
- 1 teaspoon Dijon mustard
- 1/2 teaspoon garlic powder
- 1 ½ tablespoons olive oil
- 1/2 teaspoon smoked cayenne pepper
- Salt and ground black peppercorns, to savor
- 1 cup goat cheese, shredded

Directions:
1. Set the Air Fryer to cook at 385 degrees F.
2. In a bowl, thoroughly combine all ingredients, except for cheese.
3. Dump the shrimp into the cooking basket; air-fry for 7 to 8 minutes. Bon appétit!

Peppercorn Cod

Servings: 4
Cooking Time: 15 Minutes
Ingredients:

- 4 cod fillets, boneless
- A pinch of salt and black pepper
- 1 tablespoon thyme, chopped
- ½ teaspoon black peppercorns
- 2 tablespoons olive oil
- 1 fennel, sliced
- 2 garlic cloves, minced
- 1 red bell pepper, chopped
- 2 teaspoons Italian seasoning

Directions:

1. In a bowl, mix the fennel with bell pepper and the other ingredients except the fish fillets and toss. Put this into a pan that fits the air fryer, add the fish on top, introduce the pan in your air fryer and cook at 380 degrees F for 15 minutes. Divide between plates and serve.

Sweet Honey-hoisin Glazed Salmon

Servings: 2
Cooking Time: 12 Minutes

Ingredients:

- 1 tablespoon honey
- 1 tablespoon olive oil
- 1 tablespoon rice wine
- 1 tablespoon soy sauce
- 1-lb salmon filet, cut into 2-inch rectangles
- 3 tablespoons hoisin sauce

Directions:

1. In a shallow dish, mix well all Ingredients. Marinate in the ref for 3 hours.
2. Thread salmon pieces in skewers and reserve marinade for basting. Place on skewer rack in air fryer.
3. For 12 minutes, cook on 360F. Halfway through cooking time, turnover skewers and baste with marinade. If needed, cook in batches.
4. Serve and enjoy.

Halibut Cakes With Horseradish Mayo

Servings: 4
Cooking Time: 20 Minutes

Ingredients:

- Halibut Cakes:

- 1 pound halibut
- 2 tablespoons olive oil
- 1/2 teaspoon cayenne pepper
- 1/4 teaspoon black pepper
- Salt, to taste
- 2 tablespoons cilantro, chopped
- 1 shallot, chopped
- 2 garlic cloves, minced
- 1/2 cup Romano cheese, grated
- 1/2 cup breadcrumbs
- 1 egg, whisked
- 1 tablespoon Worcestershire sauce
- Mayo Sauce:
- 1 teaspoon horseradish, grated
- 1/2 cup mayonnaise

Directions:

1. Start by preheating your Air Fryer to 380 degrees F. Spritz the Air Fryer basket with cooking oil.
2. Mix all ingredients for the halibut cakes in a bowl; knead with your hands until everything is well incorporated.
3. Shape the mixture into equally sized patties. Transfer your patties to the Air Fryer basket. Cook the fish patties for 10 minutes, turning them over halfway through.
4. Mix the horseradish and mayonnaise. Serve the halibut cakes with the horseradish mayo. Bon appétit!

Easy Grilled Pesto Scallops

Servings: 3
Cooking Time: 15 Minutes

Ingredients:

- 12 large scallops, side muscles removed
- Salt and pepper to taste
- ½ cup prepared commercial pesto

Directions:

1. Place all ingredients in a Ziploc bag and allow the scallops to marinate in the fridge for at least 2 hours.
2. Preheat the air fryer at 390F.
3. Place the grill pan accessory in the air fryer.
4. Grill the scallops for 15 minutes.
5. Serve on pasta or bread if desired.

Outrageous Crispy Fried Salmon Skin

Servings: 4

Cooking Time: 10 Minutes

Ingredients:

- ½ pound salmon skin, patted dry
- 4 tablespoons coconut oil
- Salt and pepper to taste

Directions:

1. Preheat the air fryer for 5 minutes.
2. In a large bowl, combine everything and mix well.
3. Place in the fryer basket and close.
4. Cook for 10 minutes at 400F.
5. Halfway through the cooking time, give a good shake to evenly cook the skin.

Salmon And Lime Sauce

Servings: 4

Cooking Time: 20 Minutes

Ingredients:

- 4 salmon fillets, boneless
- ¼ cup coconut cream
- 1 teaspoon lime zest, grated
- 1/3 cup heavy cream
- ¼ cup lime juice
- ½ cup coconut, shredded
- A pinch of salt and black pepper

Directions:

1. In a bowl, mix all the ingredients except the salmon and whisk. Arrange the fish in a pan that fits your air fryer, drizzle the coconut sauce all over, put the pan in the machine and cook at 360 degrees F for 20 minutes. Divide between plates and serve.

Ghee Shrimp And Green Beans

Servings: 4

Cooking Time: 15 Minutes

Ingredients:

- 1 pound shrimp, peeled and deveined
- A pinch of salt and black pepper
- ½ pound green beans, trimmed and halved
- Juice of 1 lime
- 2 tablespoons cilantro, chopped
- ¼ cup ghee, melted

Directions:

1. In a pan that fits your air fryer, mix all the ingredients, toss, introduce in the fryer and cook at 360 degrees F for 15 minutes shaking the fryer halfway. Divide into bowls and serve.

Quick 'n Easy Tuna-mac Casserole

Servings: 4

Cooking Time: 20 Minutes

Ingredients:

- 1/2 (10.75 ounce) can condensed cream of chicken soup
- 1-1/2 cups cooked macaroni
- 1/2 (5 ounce) can tuna, drained
- 1/2 cup shredded Cheddar cheese
- 3/4 cup French fried onions

Directions:

1. Lightly grease baking pan of air fryer with cooking spray.
2. Mix soup, tuna, and macaroni in pan. Sprinkle cheese on top.
3. For 15 minutes, cook on 360F.
4. Remove basket and toss the mixture a bit. Sprinkle fried onions.
5. Cook for another 5 minutes.
6. Serve and enjoy.

VEGETABLE & SIDE DISHES

Walnut & Cheese Filled Mushrooms

Servings: 4

Cooking Time: 15 Minutes

Ingredients:

- ⅓ cup walnuts, minced
- 1 tbsp canola oil
- ½ cup shredded mozzarella cheese
- 2 tbsp parsley

Directions:

1. Preheat the Air fryer to 350 F. Grease the air fryer basket with cooking spray.
2. Rub the mushrooms with the canola oil and fill them with mozzarella cheese. Top with minced walnuts and arrange on the bottom of the air fryer basket. Cook for 10 minutes until golden. Let cool for a few minutes, sprinkle with parsley, and serve.

The Best Cauliflower Tater Tots

Servings: 4

Cooking Time: 25 Minutes

Ingredients:

- 1 pound cauliflower florets
- 2 eggs
- 1 tablespoon olive oil
- 2 tablespoons scallions, chopped
- 1 garlic clove, minced
- 1 cup Colby cheese, shredded
- 1/2 cup breadcrumbs
- Sea salt and ground black pepper, to taste
- 1/4 teaspoon dried dill weed
- 1 teaspoon paprika

Directions:

1. Blanch the cauliflower in salted boiling water about 3 to 4 minutes until al dente. Drain well and pulse in a food processor.
2. Add the remaining ingredients; mix to combine well. Shape the cauliflower mixture into bite-sized tots.
3. Spritz the Air Fryer basket with cooking spray.

4. Cook in the preheated Air Fryer at 375 degrees F for 16 minutes, shaking halfway through the cooking time. Serve with your favorite sauce for dipping. Bon appétit!

Curried Eggplant Slices

Servings: 2

Cooking Time: 10 Minutes

Ingredients:

- 1 large eggplant, cut into 1/2-inch thick slices
- 1 garlic clove, minced
- 1 tbsp olive oil
- 1/2 tsp curry powder
- 1/8 tsp turmeric
- Salt

Directions:

1. Preheat the air fryer to 300 F.
2. Add all ingredients into the large mixing bowl and toss to coat.
3. Transfer eggplant slices into the air fryer basket.
4. Cook eggplant slices for 10 minutes or until lightly brown. Shake basket halfway through.
5. Serve and enjoy.

Parmesan Cauliflower Gnocchi

Servings: 4

Cooking Time: 4 Minutes

Ingredients:

- 2 cups cauliflower, boiled
- 2 oz parmesan, grated
- 1 egg yolk
- 1 teaspoon ground black pepper
- 1 teaspoon cream cheese
- 3 tablespoons coconut flour
- 1 tablespoon butter
- 1 teaspoon dried cilantro

Directions:

1. Put the boiled cauliflower in the blender and grind it until you get the smooth mixture. Then

squeeze the cauliflower to get rid of the water and transfer in the bowl. Add grated Parmesan, egg yolk, ground black pepper, cream cheese, and coconut flour. Knead the dough. Then make the log and cut it into pieces (gnocchi). Preheat the air fryer to 390F. Put the gnocchi in the air fryer in one layer and cook them for 4 minutes. Meanwhile, in the mixing bowl mix up butter and dried cilantro. Microwave the mixture until it is melted. When the gnocchi is cooked, place them in the plate and top with the melted butter mixture.

Parsley Asparagus

Servings: 4
Cooking Time: 15 Minutes
Ingredients:
- 1 pound asparagus, trimmed
- 1 fennel bulb, quartered
- A pinch of salt and black pepper
- 2 cherry tomatoes, chopped
- 2 chili peppers, chopped
- 2 tablespoons cilantro, chopped
- 2 tablespoons parsley, chopped
- 2 tablespoons olive oil
- 2 tablespoons lemon juice

Directions:
1. Heat up a pan that fits the air fryer with the oil over medium-high heat, add chili peppers and the fennel and sauté for 2 minutes. Add the rest of the ingredients, toss, put the pan in the air fryer and cook at 380 degrees F for 12 minutes. Divide everything between plates and serve.

Parmesan Squash

Servings: 6
Cooking Time: 12 Minutes
Ingredients:
- 2 lbs butternut squash, peeled and cut into 1-inch cubes
- 2 tbsp thyme, chopped
- 2 garlic cloves, minced

- 2 tbsp olive oil
- 1/2 cup parmesan cheese, grated
- 1 1/2 cups mozzarella cheese, shredded
- Pepper
- Salt

Directions:
1. Preheat the air fryer to 400 F.
2. Toss squash with thyme, garlic, and olive oil in a large bowl. Season pepper and salt.
3. Transfer squash mixture into the air fryer baking dish.
4. Place dish in the air fryer and cook squash for 10 minutes or until tender.
5. Top with parmesan and mozzarella cheese and cook for 2 minutes more or until cheese is melted.
6. Serve and enjoy.

Simple Taro Fries

Servings: 2
Cooking Time: 20 Minutes
Ingredients:
- 8 small taro, peel and cut into fries shape
- 1 tbsp olive oil
- 1/2 tsp salt

Directions:
1. Add taro slice in a bowl and toss well with olive oil and salt.
2. Transfer taro slices into the air fryer basket.
3. Cook at 360 F for 20 minutes. Toss halfway through.
4. Serve and enjoy.

Breaded Mushrooms

Servings: 4
Cooking Time: 55 Minutes
Ingredients:
- 2 cups breadcrumbs
- 2 eggs, beaten
- Salt and pepper to taste
- 2 cups Parmigiano Reggiano cheese, grated

Directions:

1. Preheat air fryer to 360 F. Pour breadcrumbs in a bowl, add salt and pepper and mix well. Pour cheese in a separate bowl. Dip each mushroom in the eggs, then in the crumbs, and then in the cheese. Slide-out the fryer basket and add 6 to 10 mushrooms. Cook for 20 minutes. Serve with cheese dip.

Zucchini Bites

Servings: 4
Cooking Time: 15 Minutes
Ingredients:
- 4 zucchinis
- 1 egg
- ½ cup parmesan cheese, grated
- 1 tbsp. Italian herbs
- 1 cup coconut, grated

Directions:
1. 1 Thinly grate the zucchini and dry with a cheesecloth, ensuring to remove all of the moisture.
2. 2 In a bowl, combine the zucchini with the egg, parmesan, Italian herbs, and grated coconut, mixing well to incorporate everything. Using your hands, mold the mixture into balls.
3. 3 Pre-heat the fryer at 400°F and place a rack inside. Lay the zucchini balls on the rack and cook for ten minutes. Serve hot.

Cinnamon Mushroom

Servings: 4
Cooking Time: 15 Minutes
Ingredients:
- 1 pound brown mushrooms
- 1 teaspoon olive oil
- 4 garlic cloves, minced
- ½ teaspoon turmeric powder
- ¼ teaspoon cinnamon powder
- Salt and black pepper to the taste

Directions:
1. In a bowl, combine all the ingredients and toss. Put the mushrooms in your air fryer's basket and

cook at 370 degrees F for 15 minutes. Divide the mix between plates and serve as a side dish.

Easy Sweet Potato Hash Browns

Servings: 2
Cooking Time: 50 Minutes
Ingredients:
- 1 pound sweet potatoes, peeled and grated
- 2 eggs, whisked
- 1/4 cup scallions, chopped
- 1 teaspoon fresh garlic, minced
- Sea salt and ground black pepper, to taste
- 1/4 teaspoon ground allspice
- 1/2 teaspoon cinnamon
- 1 tablespoon peanut oil

Directions:
1. Allow the sweet potatoes to soak for 25 minutes in cold water. Drain the water; dry the sweet potatoes with a kitchen towel.
2. Add the remaining ingredients and stir to combine well.
3. Cook in the preheated Air Fryer at 395 degrees F for 20 minutes. Shake the basket once or twice. Serve with ketchup.

Okra Salad

Servings: 2
Cooking Time: 6 Minutes
Ingredients:
- 6 oz okra, sliced
- 3 oz green beans, chopped
- 1 cup arugula, chopped
- 1 teaspoon lemon juice
- 1 teaspoon olive oil
- ½ teaspoon salt
- 2 eggs, beaten
- 1 tablespoon coconut flakes
- Cooking spray

Directions:

1. In the mixing bowl mix up sliced okra and green beans. Add cooking spray and salt and mix up the mixture well. Then add beaten eggs and shake it. After this, sprinkle the vegetables with coconut flakes and shake okra and green beans to coat them in the coconut flakes. Preheat the air fryer to 400F. Put the vegetable mixture in the air fryer and cook it for 6 minutes. Shake the mixture after 3 minutes of cooking. After this, mix up cooked vegetables with arugula, lemon juice, and sprinkle with olive oil. Shake the salad.

Collard Greens And Bacon Recipe

Servings: 4
Cooking Time: 22 Minutes
Ingredients:

- 1 lb. collard greens
- 1 tbsp. apple cider vinegar
- 2 tbsp. chicken stock
- 3 bacon strips; chopped
- 1/4 cup cherry tomatoes; halved
- Salt and black pepper to the taste

Directions:

1. Heat up a pan that fits your air fryer over medium heat, add bacon; stir and cook 1-2 minutes
2. Add tomatoes, collard greens, vinegar, stock, salt and pepper; stir, introduce in your air fryer and cook at 320 °F, for 10 minutes. Divide among plates and serve

Butter Broccoli

Servings: 4
Cooking Time: 15 Minutes
Ingredients:

- 1 pound broccoli florets
- A pinch of salt and black pepper
- 1 teaspoons sweet paprika
- ½ tablespoon butter, melted

Directions:

1. In a bowl, mix the broccoli with the rest of the ingredients, and toss. Put the broccoli in your air

fryer's basket, cook at 350 degrees F for 15 minutes, divide between plates and serve.

Cheese-crusted Brussels Sprouts

Servings: 4
Cooking Time: 20 Minutes
Ingredients:

- 2 tbsp canola oil
- 3 tbsp breadcrumbs
- 1 tbsp paprika
- 2 tbsp Grana Padano cheese, grated
- 2 tbsp sage, chopped

Directions:

1. Preheat the Air fryer to 400 F. Line the air fryer basket with parchment paper.
2. In a bowl, mix breadcrumbs and paprika with Grana Padano cheese. Drizzle the Brussels sprouts with the canola oil and pour in the breadcrumb/cheese mixture; toss to coat. Place in the air fryer basket and cook for 15 minutes, shaking it every 4-5 minutes. Serve sprinkled with chopped sage.

Green Celery Puree

Servings: 6
Cooking Time: 6 Minutes
Ingredients:

- 1-pound celery stalks, chopped
- ½ cup spinach, chopped
- 2 oz Parmesan, grated
- ¼ cup chicken broth
- ½ teaspoon cayenne pepper

Directions:

1. In the air fryer pan, mix celery stalk with chopped spinach, chicken broth, and cayenne pepper. Blend the mixture until homogenous. After this, top the puree with Parmesan. Preheat the air fryer to 400F. Put the pan with puree in the air fryer basket and cook the meal for 6 minutes.

Cheese Lings

Servings: 6
Cooking Time: 25 Minutes
Ingredients:
- 1 cup flour
- small cubes cheese, grated
- ¼ tsp. chili powder
- 1 tsp. butter
- Salt to taste
- 1 tsp. baking powder

Directions:
1. Combine all the ingredients to form a dough, along with a small amount water as necessary.
2. Divide the dough into equal portions and roll each one into a ball.
3. Pre-heat Air Fryer at 360°F.
4. Transfer the balls to the fryer and air fry for 5 minutes, stirring periodically.

Mustard Garlic Asparagus

Servings: 4
Cooking Time: 12 Minutes
Ingredients:
- 1 pound asparagus, trimmed
- 2 tablespoons olive oil
- ¼ cup mustard
- 3 garlic cloves, minced
- ½ cup parmesan, grated

Directions:
1. In a bowl, mix the asparagus with the oil, garlic and mustard and toss really well. Put the asparagus spears in your air fryer's basket and cook at 400 degrees F for 12 minutes. Divide between plates, sprinkle the parmesan on top and serve.

Roasted Cauliflower & Broccoli

Servings: 6
Cooking Time: 15 Minutes
Ingredients:
- 3 cups cauliflower florets
- 3 cups broccoli florets
- 1/4 tsp paprika
- 1/2 tsp garlic powder
- 2 tbsp olive oil
- 1/8 tsp pepper
- 1/4 tsp sea salt

Directions:
1. Preheat the air fryer to 400 F.
2. Add broccoli in microwave-safe bowl and microwave for 3 minutes. Drain well.
3. Add broccoli in a large mixing bowl. Add remaining ingredients and toss well.
4. Transfer broccoli and cauliflower mixture into the air fryer basket and cook for 12 minutes.
5. Toss halfway through.
6. Serve and enjoy.

Radishes And Spring Onions Mix

Servings: 4
Cooking Time: 15 Minutes
Ingredients:
- 20 radishes, halved
- 1 tablespoon olive oil
- 3 green onions, chopped
- Salt and black pepper to the taste
- 3 teaspoons black sesame seeds
- 2 tablespoons olive oil

Directions:
1. In a bowl, mix all the ingredients and toss well. Put the radishes in your air fryer's basket, cook at 400 degrees F for 15 minutes, divide between plates and serve as a side dish.

Creamy Cauliflower Tots

Servings: 4
Cooking Time: 8 Minutes
Ingredients:
- 1 teaspoon cream cheese
- 5 oz Monterey Jack cheese, shredded
- 1 cup cauliflower, chopped, boiled

- ¼ teaspoon garlic powder
- 1 teaspoon sunflower oil

Directions:

1. Put the boiled cauliflower in the blender. Add garlic powder, cream cheese, and shredded Monterey Jack cheese. Blend the mixture until smooth. Make the cauliflower tots and refrigerate them for 10 minutes. Meanwhile, preheat the air fryer to 365F. Place the cauliflower inside the air fryer basket and sprinkle with sunflower oil. Cook the tots for 4 minutes from each side.

Avocado And Green Beans

Servings: 4
Cooking Time: 15 Minutes
Ingredients:

- 1 pint mixed cherry tomatoes, halved
- 1 avocado, peeled, pitted and cubed
- ¼ pound green beans, trimmed and halved
- 2 tablespoons olive oil

Directions:

1. In a pan that fits your air fryer, mix the tomatoes with the rest of the ingredients, toss, put the pan in the machine and cook at 360 degrees F for 15 minutes. Transfer to bowls and serve.

Broccoli Hash Recipe

Servings: 2
Cooking Time: 38 Minutes
Ingredients:

- 10 oz. mushrooms; halved
- 1 broccoli head; florets separated
- 1 garlic clove; minced
- 1 tbsp. balsamic vinegar
- 1 avocado; peeled and pitted
- A pinch of red pepper flakes
- 1 yellow onion; chopped.
- 1 tbsp. olive oil
- Salt and black pepper
- 1 tsp. basil; dried

Directions:

1. In a bowl; mix mushrooms with broccoli, onion, garlic and avocado.
2. In another bowl, mix vinegar, oil, salt, pepper and basil and whisk well
3. Pour this over veggies, toss to coat, leave aside for 30 minutes; transfer to your air fryer's basket and cook at 350 °F, for 8 minutes; Divide among plates and serve with pepper flakes on top

Potato Casserole Dish

Servings: 4
Cooking Time: 55 Minutes
Ingredients:

- 3 lbs. sweet potatoes; scrubbed
- 1/4 cup milk
- 2 tbsp. white flour
- 1/4 tsp. allspice; ground
- 1/2 tsp. nutmeg; ground
- Salt to the taste
- For the topping:
- 1/2 cup almond flour
- 1/2 cup walnuts; soaked, drained and ground
- 1/4 cup sugar
- 1 tsp. cinnamon powder
- 5 tbsp. butter
- 1/4 cup pecans; soaked, drained and ground
- 1/4 cup coconut; shredded
- 1 tbsp. chia seeds

Directions:

1. Place potatoes in your air fryer's basket, prick them with a fork and cook at 360 °F, for 30 minutes.
2. Meanwhile; in a bowl, mix almond flour with pecans, walnuts, 1/4 cup coconut, 1/4 cup sugar, chia seeds, 1 tsp. cinnamon and the butter and stir everything.
3. Transfer potatoes to a cutting board, cool them, peel and place them in a baking dish that fits your air fryer.
4. Add milk, flour, salt, nutmeg and allspice and stir

5. Add crumble mix you've made earlier on top; place dish in your air fryer's basket and cook at 400 °F, for 8 minutes. Divide among plates and serve as a side dish.

Fried Peppers With Sriracha Mayo

Servings: 2
Cooking Time: 20 Minutes
Ingredients:
- 4 bell peppers, seeded and sliced (1-inch pieces)
- 1 onion, sliced (1-inch pieces)
- 1 tablespoon olive oil
- 1/2 teaspoon dried rosemary
- 1/2 teaspoon dried basil
- Kosher salt, to taste
- 1/4 teaspoon ground black pepper
- 1/3 cup mayonnaise
- 1/3 teaspoon Sriracha

Directions:
1. Toss the bell peppers and onions with the olive oil, rosemary, basil, salt, and black pepper.
2. Place the peppers and onions on an even layer in the cooking basket. Cook at 400 degrees F for 12 to 14 minutes.
3. Meanwhile, make the sauce by whisking the mayonnaise and Sriracha. Serve immediately.

Cauliflower Patties

Servings: 2
Cooking Time: 10 Minutes
Ingredients:
- ¼ cup cauliflower, shredded
- 1 egg yolk
- ½ teaspoon ground turmeric
- ¼ teaspoon onion powder
- ¼ teaspoon salt
- 2 oz Cheddar cheese, shredded
- ¼ teaspoon baking powder
- 1 teaspoon heavy cream
- 1 tablespoon coconut flakes

- Cooking spray

Directions:
1. Squeeze the shredded cauliflower and put it in the bowl. Add egg yolk, ground turmeric, onion powder, baking powder, salt, heavy cream, and coconut flakes. Then melt Cheddar cheese and add it in the cauliflower mixture. Stir the ingredients until you get the smooth mass. After this, make the medium size cauliflower patties. Preheat the air fryer to 365F. Spray the air fryer basket with cooking spray and put the patties inside. Cook them for 5 minutes from each side.

Spinach Mash

Servings: 4
Cooking Time: 13 Minutes
Ingredients:
- 3 cups spinach, chopped
- ½ cup Mozzarella, shredded
- 4 bacon slices, chopped
- 1 teaspoon butter
- 1 cup heavy cream
- ½ teaspoon salt
- ½ jalapeno pepper, chopped

Directions:
1. Place the bacon in the air fryer and cook it for 8 minutes at 400F. Stir it from time to time with the help of the spatula. After this, put the cooked bacon in the air fryer casserole mold. Add heavy cream spinach, jalapeno pepper, salt, butter, and Mozzarella. Stir it gently. Cook the mash for 5 minutes at 400F. Then stir the spinach mash carefully with the help of the spoon.

Pecorino Zucchini

Servings: 5
Cooking Time: 5 Minutes
Ingredients:
- 1 large zucchini
- 2 cherry tomatoes, chopped
- 1 bell pepper, diced

- 3 spring onions, diced
- 1 tablespoon sesame oil
- 4 oz Pecorino cheese, grated
- ½ teaspoon chili flakes
- ¼ teaspoon minced garlic
- 1 teaspoon flax seeds

Directions:

1. Make the spirals from the zucchini with the help of the spiralizer and sprinkle with sesame oil. Then place them in the air fryer, add diced bell pepper, and cook for 5 minutes at 355F. After this, transfer the cooked vegetables in the big bowl. Add cherry tomatoes, spring onions, Pecorino, chili flakes, minced garlic, and flax seeds. Mix up zucchini Primavera with the help of 2 spatulas.

Squash Fritters

Servings: 4
Cooking Time: 7 Minutes
Ingredients:

- 1 yellow summer squash, grated
- 1 egg, lightly beaten
- 3 oz cream cheese
- 2 tbsp olive oil
- 1/2 tsp dried oregano
- 1/4 cup almond flour
- 1/3 cup carrot, grated
- Pepper
- Salt

Directions:

1. Spray air fryer basket with cooking spray.
2. Add all ingredients into the mixing bowl and mix until well combined.
3. Make patties from bowl mixture and place into the air fryer basket and cook at 400 F for 7 minutes.
4. Serve and enjoy.

Roasted Broccoli With Sesame Seeds

Servings: 2
Cooking Time: 15 Minutes

Ingredients:

- 1 pound broccoli florets
- 2 tablespoons sesame oil
- 1/2 teaspoon shallot powder
- 1/2 teaspoon porcini powder
- 1 teaspoon garlic powder
- Sea salt and ground black pepper, to taste
- 1/2 teaspoon cumin powder
- 1/4 teaspoon paprika
- 2 tablespoons sesame seeds

Directions:

1. Start by preheating the Air Fryer to 400 degrees F.
2. Blanch the broccoli in salted boiling water until al dente, about 3 to 4 minutes. Drain well and transfer to the lightly greased Air Fryer basket.
3. Add the sesame oil, shallot powder, porcini powder, garlic powder, salt, black pepper, cumin powder, paprika, and sesame seeds.
4. Cook for 6 minutes, tossing halfway through the cooking time. Bon appétit!

Mini Cheese Scones

Servings: 10
Cooking Time: 25 Minutes
Ingredients:

- Salt and pepper to taste
- ¾ oz butter
- 1 tsp chives
- 1 whole egg
- 1 tbsp milk
- 2 ¾ cheddar cheese, shredded

Directions:

1. Preheat your air fryer to 340 F. In a bowl, mix butter, flour, cheddar cheese, chives, milk and egg to get a sticky dough. Dust a flat surface with flour. Roll the dough into small balls. Place the balls in your air fryer's cooking basket and cook for 20 minutes. Serve and enjoy!

Balsamic Root Vegetables

Servings: 3

Cooking Time: 25 Minutes

Ingredients:

- 2 potatoes, cut into 1 1/2-inch pieces
- 2 carrots, cut into 1 1/2-inch pieces
- 2 parsnips, cut into 1 1/2-inch pieces
- 1 onion, cut into 1 1/2-inch pieces
- Pink Himalayan salt and ground black pepper, to taste
- 1/4 teaspoon smoked paprika
- 1 teaspoon garlic powder
- 1/2 teaspoon dried thyme
- 1/2 teaspoon dried marjoram
- 2 tablespoons olive oil
- 2 tablespoons balsamic vinegar

Directions:

1. Toss all ingredients in a large mixing dish.
2. Roast in the preheated Air Fryer at 400 degrees F for 10 minutes. Shake the basket and cook for 7 minutes more.
3. Serve with some extra fresh herbs if desired. Bon appétit!

Best Roasted Broccoli

Servings: 2

Cooking Time: 15 Minutes

Ingredients:

- 2 cups broccoli florets
- 2 tablespoons yogurt
- 1 tablespoon chickpea flour
- ¼ teaspoons turmeric powder
- ½ teaspoon salt
- ¼ teaspoon chaat masala

Directions:

1. Place all ingredients in a bowl and toss to combine.
2. Place the baking dish accessory into the air fryer and place the food into the dish.
3. Close the air fryer and cook for 15 minutes at 350F.

4. Halfway through the cooking time, give the baking dish a good shake.

Cauliflower Tots

Servings: 8

Cooking Time: 20 Minutes

Ingredients:

- 1 large head cauliflower
- ½ cup parmesan cheese, grated
- 1 cup mozzarella cheese, shredded
- 1 tsp. seasoned salt
- 1 egg

Directions:

1. Place a steamer basket over a pot of boiling water, ensuring the water is not high enough to enter the basket.
2. Cut up the cauliflower into florets and transfer to the steamer basket. Cover the pot with a lid and leave to steam for seven minutes, making sure the cauliflower softens.
3. Place the florets on a cheesecloth and leave to cool. Remove as much moisture as possible. This is crucial as it ensures the cauliflower will harden.
4. In a bowl, break up the cauliflower with a fork.
5. Stir in the parmesan, mozzarella, seasoned salt, and egg, incorporating the cauliflower well with all of the other ingredients. Make sure the mixture is firm enough to be moldable.
6. Using your hand, mold about two tablespoons of the mixture into tots and repeat until you have used up all of the mixture. Put each tot into your air fryer basket. They may need to be cooked in multiple batches.
7. Cook at 320°F for twelve minutes, turning them halfway through. Ensure they are brown in color before serving.

Collard Greens Sauté

Servings: 4

Cooking Time: 12 Minutes

Ingredients:

- 1 pound collard greens, trimmed
- 2 fennel bulbs, trimmed and quartered
- 2 tablespoons olive oil
- Salt and black pepper to the taste
- ½ cup keto tomato sauce

Directions:

1. In a pan that fits your air fryer, mix the collard greens with the fennel and the rest of the ingredients, toss, put the pan in the fryer and cook at 350 degrees F for 12 minutes. Divide everything between plates and serve.

Crispy Parmesan Asparagus

Servings: 4
Cooking Time: 20 Minutes

Ingredients:

- 2 eggs
- 1 teaspoon Dijon mustard
- 1 cup Parmesan cheese, grated
- 1 cup bread crumbs
- Sea salt and ground black pepper, to taste
- 18 asparagus spears, trimmed
- 1/2 cup sour cream

Directions:

1. Start by preheating your Air Fryer to 400 degrees F.
2. In a shallow bowl, whisk the eggs and mustard. In another shallow bowl, combine the Parmesan cheese, breadcrumbs, salt, and black pepper.
3. Dip the asparagus spears in the egg mixture, then in the parmesan mixture; press to adhere.
4. Cook for 5 minutes; work in three batches. Serve with sour cream on the side. Enjoy!

Coconut Mushrooms Mix

Servings: 4
Cooking Time: 15 Minutes

Ingredients:

- 1 pound brown mushrooms, sliced
- 1 pound kale, torn

- Salt and black pepper to the taste
- 2 tablespoons olive oil
- 14 ounces coconut milk

Directions:

1. In a pan that fits your air fryer, mix the kale with the rest of the ingredients and toss. Put the pan in the fryer, cook at 380 degrees F for 15 minutes, divide between plates and serve.

Roasted Broccoli

Servings: 4
Cooking Time: 7 Minutes

Ingredients:

- 4 cups broccoli florets
- 1/4 cup water
- 1 tbsp olive oil
- 1/4 tsp pepper
- 1/8 tsp kosher salt

Directions:

1. Add broccoli, oil, pepper, and salt in a bowl and toss well.
2. Add 1/4 cup of water into the bottom of air fryer (under the basket).
3. Transfer broccoli into the air fryer basket and cook for 7 minutes at 400 F.
4. Serve and enjoy.

Cheesy Crusted Baked Eggplant

Servings: 3
Cooking Time: 45 Minutes

Ingredients:

- 1 pound eggplant, sliced
- 1 tablespoon sea salt
- 1/4 cup Romano cheese, preferably freshly grated
- 1/3 cup breadcrumbs
- Sea salt and cracked black pepper, to taste
- 1 egg, whisked
- 4 tablespoons cornmeal
- 1/4 cup mozzarella cheese, grated

- 2 tablespoons fresh Italian parsley, roughly chopped

Directions:

1. Toss the eggplant with 1 tablespoon of salt and let it stand for 30 minutes. Drain and rinse.
2. Mix the cheese, breadcrumbs, salt, and black pepper in a bowl. Then, add the whisked egg and cornmeal.
3. Dip the eggplant slices in the batter and press to coat on all sides. Transfer to the lightly greased Air Fryer basket.
4. Cook at 370 degrees F for 7 to 9 minutes. Turn each slice over and top with the mozzarella. Cook an additional 2 minutes or until the cheese melts.
5. Serve garnished with fresh Italian parsley. Bon appétit!

Ginger Paneer

Servings: 4
Cooking Time: 6 Minutes
Ingredients:

- 1 cup paneer, cubed
- 1 tomato
- 2 spring onions, chopped
- ½ teaspoon ground coriander
- 1 tablespoon lemon juice
- ½ teaspoon fresh cilantro, chopped
- 1 tablespoon mustard oil
- ¼ teaspoon ginger paste
- ½ teaspoon minced garlic
- ½ teaspoon red chili powder
- ¼ teaspoon garam masala powder
- ¼ teaspoon salt

Directions:

1. Chop the tomato on 4 cubes. Then chop the onion on 4 cubes too. Sprinkle the paneer with ground coriander, lemon juice, cilantro, mustard oil, ginger paste, minced garlic, red chili powder, garam masala, and salt. Massage the paneer cubes with the help of the fingertips to coat them well. After this, string the paneer cubes, tomato, and onion on the skewers. Preheat the air fryer to 385F. Place the paneer tikka skewers in the air fryer basket and cook them for 3 minutes from each side.

Plums & Pancetta Bombs

Servings: 10
Cooking Time: 25 Minutes
Ingredients:

- 2 tbsp fresh rosemary, finely chopped
- 1 cup almonds, chopped into small pieces
- Salt and black pepper
- 15 dried plums, chopped
- 15 pancetta slices

Directions:

1. Line the air fryer basket with baking paper. In a bowl, add cheese, rosemary, almonds, salt, pepper and plums; stir well. Roll into balls and wrap with a pancetta slice. Arrange the bombs on the fryer and cook for 10 minutes at 400 F. Let cool before removing them from the air fryer. Serve with toothpicks.

Coriander Leeks

Servings: 6
Cooking Time: 10 Minutes
Ingredients:

- 10 oz leek, chopped
- 2 tablespoons ricotta
- 1 tablespoon butter, melted
- 1 teaspoon ground coriander
- ¼ teaspoon salt

Directions:

1. Sprinkle the leek with salt and ground coriander and transfer in the air fryer. Add butter and gently stir the ingredients. After this, cook the leek for 5 minutes at 375F. Stir the vegetables well and add ricotta. Cook the meal for 5 minutes more. Serve the cooked leek with ricotta gravy.

Tater Tots For Two

Servings: 2

Cooking Time: 20 Minutes

Ingredients:

- 2 cups frozen tater tots
- ½ teaspoon cooking oil

Directions:

1. Place all ingredients into the air fryer baking dish. Toss to coat the tater tots in the oil.
2. Close the air fryer and cook for 20 minutes at 350F.
3. Halfway through the cooking time, give the baking dish a good shake.

Zucchini Parmesan Chips

Servings: 3

Cooking Time: 15 Minutes

Ingredients:

- 1 cup breadcrumbs
- 2 eggs, beaten
- 1 cup grated Parmesan cheese
- Salt and pepper to taste
- 1 tsp smoked paprika

Directions:

1. In a bowl, add breadcrumbs, salt, pepper, cheese, and paprika. Mix well. Dip zucchini slices in eggs and then in the cheese mix while pressing to coat them well. Spray the coated slices with cooking spray and put the in the fryer basket. Cook at 350 F for 8 minutes. Serve with salt spicy dip.

Crumbed Beans

Servings: 4

Cooking Time: 10 Minutes

Ingredients:

- ½ cup flour
- 1 tsp. smoky chipotle powder
- ½ tsp. ground black pepper
- 1 tsp. sea salt flakes
- 2 eggs, beaten

- ½ cup crushed saltines
- 10 oz. wax beans

Directions:

1. Combine the flour, chipotle powder, black pepper, and salt in a bowl. Put the eggs in a second bowl. Place the crushed saltines in a third bowl.
2. Wash the beans with cold water and discard any tough strings.
3. Coat the beans with the flour mixture, before dipping them into the beaten egg. Lastly cover them with the crushed saltines.
4. Spritz the beans with a cooking spray.
5. Air-fry at 360°F for 4 minutes. Give the cooking basket a good shake and continue to cook for 3 minutes. Serve hot.

Asparagus And Green Beans Salad

Servings: 3

Cooking Time: 6 Minutes

Ingredients:

- 3 oz asparagus, chopped
- 2 oz green beans, chopped
- 1 cup arugula, chopped
- 1 tablespoon hazelnuts, chopped
- 1 teaspoon flax seeds
- 2 oz Mozzarella, chopped
- 1 tablespoon olive oil
- ½ teaspoon salt
- ½ teaspoon ground paprika
- ½ teaspoon ground black pepper
- Cooking spray

Directions:

1. Preheat the air fryer to 400F. Put the asparagus and green beans in the air fryer and spray them with cooking spray. Cook the vegetables for 6 minutes at 400F. Shake the vegetables after 3 minutes of cooking. Then cool them to the room temperature and put in the salad bowl. Add hazelnuts, flax seeds, chopped Mozzarella, salt, ground paprika, and ground black pepper. Sprinkle the salad with olive oil and shake well.

Turmeric Cauliflower

Servings: 4

Cooking Time: 8 Minutes

Ingredients:

- 1-pound cauliflower head
- 1 tablespoon ground turmeric
- 1 tablespoon coconut oil
- ½ teaspoon dried cilantro
- ¼ teaspoon salt

Directions:

1. Slice the cauliflower head on 4 steaks. Then rub every cauliflower steak with dried cilantro, salt, and ground turmeric. Sprinkle the steaks with coconut oil. Preheat the air fryer to 400F. Place the cauliflower steaks in the air fryer basket and cook for 4 minutes from each side.

Cheesy Rutabaga

Servings: 2

Cooking Time: 8 Minutes

Ingredients:

- 6 oz rutabaga, chopped
- 2 oz Jarlsberg cheese, grated
- 1 tablespoon butter
- ½ teaspoon dried parsley
- ½ teaspoon salt
- ½ teaspoon minced garlic
- 3 tablespoons heavy cream

Directions:

1. In the mixing bowl mix up a rutabaga, dried parsley, salt, and minced garlic. Then add heavy cream and mix up the vegetables well. After this, preheat the air fryer to 375F. Put the rutabaga mixture in the air fryer and cook it for 6 minutes. Then stir it well and top with grated cheese. Cook the meal for 2 minutes more. Transfer the cooked rutabaga in the plates and top with butter.

Mustard Cabbage

Servings: 4

Cooking Time: 40 Minutes

Ingredients:

- 1-pound white cabbage
- 1 teaspoon mustard
- 1 teaspoon ground black pepper
- ½ teaspoon salt
- 3 tablespoons butter, melted
- ½ teaspoon ground paprika
- ½ teaspoon chili flakes
- 1 teaspoon dried thyme

Directions:

1. In the mixing bowl mix up mustard, ground black pepper, salt, butter, ground paprika, chili flakes, and dried thyme. Brush the cabbage with the mustard mixture generously and place it in the air fryer. Cook the cabbage for 40 minutes at 365F. Then cool the cooked vegetable to the room temperature and slice into servings.

Cheese Stuffed Roasted Peppers

Servings: 2

Cooking Time: 20 Minutes

Ingredients:

- 2 red bell peppers, tops and seeds removed
- 2 yellow bell peppers, tops and seeds removed
- Salt and pepper, to taste
- 1 cup cream cheese
- 4 tablespoons mayonnaise
- 2 pickles, chopped

Directions:

1. Arrange the peppers in the lightly greased cooking basket. Cook in the preheated Air Fryer at 400 degrees F for 15 minutes, turning them over halfway through the cooking time.

2. Season with salt and pepper.

3. Then, in a mixing bowl, combine the cream cheese with the mayonnaise and chopped pickles. Stuff the pepper with the cream cheese mixture and serve. Enjoy!

Sweet Corn Fritters

Servings: 4
Cooking Time: 20 Minutes
Ingredients:
- 1 medium-sized carrot, grated
- 1 yellow onion, finely chopped
- 4 oz. canned sweet corn kernels, drained
- 1 tsp. sea salt flakes
- 1 heaping tbsp. fresh cilantro, chopped
- 1 medium-sized egg, whisked
- 2 tbsp. plain milk
- 1 cup of Parmesan cheese, grated
- ¼ cup flour
- ⅓ tsp. baking powder
- ⅓ tsp. sugar

Directions:
1. Place the grated carrot in a colander and press down to squeeze out any excess moisture. Dry it with a paper towel.
2. Combine the carrots with the remaining ingredients.
3. Mold 1 tablespoon of the mixture into a ball and press it down with your hand or a spoon to flatten it. Repeat until the rest of the mixture is used up.
4. Spritz the balls with cooking spray.
5. Arrange in the basket of your Air Fryer, taking care not to overlap any balls. Cook at 350°F for 8 to 11 minutes or until they're firm.
6. Serve warm.

Balsamic And Garlic Cabbage Mix

Servings: 4
Cooking Time: 15 Minutes
Ingredients:
- 4 garlic cloves, minced
- 1 tablespoon olive oil
- 6 cups red cabbage, shredded
- 1 tablespoon balsamic vinegar
- Salt and black pepper to the taste

Directions:

1. In a pan that fits the air fryer, combine all the ingredients, toss, introduce the pan in the air fryer and cook at 380 degrees F for 15 minutes. Divide between plates and serve as a side dish.

Zucchini Nests

Servings: 6
Cooking Time: 6 Minutes
Ingredients:
- 10 oz zucchini, grated
- 4 quail eggs
- 1 tablespoon coconut flour
- 1 oz Parmesan, grated
- ¼ teaspoon cayenne pepper
- 1 teaspoon butter, melted

Directions:
1. Brush the muffin molds with butter. Then mix up cayenne pepper and grated zucchini. Put the vegetable mixture in the muffin molds and flatten it in the shape of the nests. After this, crack the quail eggs in the nests and sprinkle with grated Parmesan. Preheat the air fryer to 390F. Put the muffin molds with nests in the air fryer basket and cook for 6 minutes.

Asian Cauliflower Rice With Eggs

Servings: 4
Cooking Time: 20 Minutes
Ingredients:
- 2 cups cauliflower, food-processed into rice-like particles
- 2 tablespoons peanut oil
- 1/2 cup scallions, chopped
- 2 bell pepper, chopped
- 4 eggs, beaten
- Sea salt and ground black pepper, to taste
- 1/2 teaspoon granulated garlic

Directions:
1. Grease a baking pan with nonstick cooking spray.

2. Add the cauliflower rice and the other ingredients to the baking pan.

3. Cook at 400 degrees F for 12 minutes, checking occasionally to ensure even cooking. Enjoy!

Air Fried Green Tomatoes

Servings: 1

Cooking Time: 7 Minutes

Ingredients:

- ½ cup panko breadcrumbs
- 3 tablespoons cornstarch
- ½ teaspoon dried basil, ground
- ½ teaspoon dried oregano, ground
- ½ teaspoon granulated onion
- Salt and pepper, to taste
- 1 medium-sized green tomato, sliced
- ½ teaspoon cooking oil

Directions:

1. In a mixing bowl, combine the panko breadcrumbs, cornstarch, basil, oregano, onion, salt, and pepper.

2. Dredge the tomato slices in the breadcrumb mixture.

3. Brush with oil and arrange on the double layer rack.

4. Place the rack with the dredged tomato slices in the air fryer.

5. Close the lid and cook for 7 minutes at 350F.

Butter Fennel

Servings: 4

Cooking Time: 12 Minutes

Ingredients:

- 2 big fennel bulbs, sliced
- 2 tablespoons butter, melted
- Salt and black pepper to the taste
- ½ cup coconut cream

Directions:

1. In a pan that fits the air fryer, combine all the ingredients, toss, introduce in the machine and cook

at 370 degrees F for 12 minutes. Divide between plates and serve as a side dish.

Tomato Artichokes Mix

Servings: 4

Cooking Time: 15 Minutes

Ingredients:

- 14 ounces artichoke hearts, drained
- 1 tablespoon olive oil
- 2 cups black olives, pitted
- 3 garlic cloves, minced
- ½ cup keto tomato sauce
- 1 teaspoon garlic powder

Directions:

1. In a pan that fits your air fryer, mix the olives with the artichokes and the other ingredients, toss, put the pan in the fryer and cook at 350 degrees F for 15 minutes. Divide the mix between plates and serve.

Garlic Stuffed Mushrooms

Servings: 4

Cooking Time: 25 Minutes

Ingredients:

- 6 small mushrooms
- 1 oz. onion, peeled and diced
- 1 tbsp. friendly bread crumbs
- 1 tbsp. olive oil
- 1 tsp. garlic, pureed
- 1 tsp. parsley
- Salt and pepper to taste

Directions:

1. Combine the bread crumbs, oil, onion, parsley, salt, pepper and garlic in a bowl. Cut out the mushrooms' stalks and stuff each cap with the crumb mixture.

2. Cook in the Air Fryer for 10 minutes at 350°F.

3. Serve with a side of mayo dip.

Tamari Eggplant

Servings: 6
Cooking Time: 30 Minutes
Ingredients:
- 3 eggplants, trimmed
- 1 teaspoon tamari sauce
- 1 tablespoon olive oil
- 1 teaspoon liquid stevia
- ½ teaspoon liquid smoke
- ½ teaspoon smoked paprika
- ¼ teaspoon cayenne pepper
- ¼ teaspoon salt

Directions:
1. Slice the eggplants on the long pieces. In the mixing bowl mix up tamari sauce, olive oil, liquid stevia, liquid smoke, smoked paprika, cayenne pepper, and salt. Then brush every eggplant piece with tamari sauce mixture. Preheat the air fryer to 400F. Put the eggplant bacon (pieces) in the air fryer in one layer and cook them for 4 minutes from each side or until the eggplant slices are light crunchy. Cook the remaining eggplant bacon.

Greek-style Vegetable Bake

Servings: 4
Cooking Time: 35 Minutes
Ingredients:
- 1 eggplant, peeled and sliced
- 2 bell peppers, seeded and sliced
- 1 red onion, sliced
- 1 teaspoon fresh garlic, minced
- 4 tablespoons olive oil
- 1 teaspoon mustard
- 1 teaspoon dried oregano
- 1 teaspoon smoked paprika
- Salt and ground black pepper, to taste
- 1 tomato, sliced
- 6 ounces halloumi cheese, sliced lengthways

Directions:

1. Start by preheating your Air Fryer to 370 degrees F. Spritz a baking pan with nonstick cooking spray.
2. Place the eggplant, peppers, onion, and garlic on the bottom of the baking pan. Add the olive oil, mustard, and spices. Transfer to the cooking basket and cook for 14 minutes.
3. Top with the tomatoes and cheese; increase the temperature to 390 degrees F and cook for 5 minutes more until bubbling. Let it sit on a cooling rack for 10 minutes before serving.
4. Bon appétit!

Italian-style Eggplant With Mozzarella Cheese

Servings: 4
Cooking Time: 45 Minutes
Ingredients:
- 1 pound eggplant, sliced
- 1 tablespoon sea salt
- 1/2 cup Romano cheese, preferably freshly grated
- Sea salt and cracked black pepper, to taste
- 1 egg, whisked
- 4 ounces pork rinds
- 1/2 cup mozzarella cheese, grated
- 2 tablespoons fresh Italian parsley, roughly chopped

Directions:
1. Toss the eggplant with 1 tablespoon of salt and let it stand for 30 minutes. Drain and rinse.
2. Mix the cheese, salt, and black pepper in a bowl. Then, add the whisked egg.
3. Dip the eggplant slices in the batter and press to coat on all sides. Roll them over pork rinds. Transfer to the lightly greased Air Fryer basket.
4. Cook at 370 degrees F for 7 to 9 minutes. Turn each slice over and top with the mozzarella. Cook an additional 2 minutes or until the cheese melts.
5. Serve garnished with fresh Italian parsley. Bon appétit!

Basil Zucchini Noodles

Servings: 4

Cooking Time: 15 Minutes

Ingredients:

- 4 zucchinis, cut with a spiralizer
- 1 tablespoon olive oil
- 4 garlic cloves, minced
- 1 and ½ cups tomatoes, crushed
- Salt and black pepper to the taste
- 1 tablespoon basil, chopped
- ¼ cup green onions, chopped

Directions:

1. In a pan that fits your air fryer, mix zucchini noodles with the other ingredients, toss, introduce in the fryer and cook at 380 degrees F for 15 minutes. Divide between plates and serve as a side dish.

VEGAN & VEGETARIAN RECIPES

Root Vegetable Medley

Servings: 4

Cooking Time: 30 Minutes

Ingredients:

- 2 carrots, sliced
- 1 turnip, peeled and cut into chunks
- 1 rutabaga, peeled and cut into chunks
- 2 potatoes, peeled and cut into chunks
- 1 beet, peeled and cut into chunks
- Salt and black pepper to taste
- 2 tbsp fresh thyme, chopped
- 2 tbsp olive oil
- 2 tbsp tomato pesto

Directions:

1. Preheat the Air fryer to 400 F.
2. In a bowl, combine all the root vegetables, salt, pepper, and olive oil. Toss to coat and transfer to air fryer basket. Cook for 12 minutes, then shake and continue cooking for another 10 minutes. Combine the pesto with 2 tbsp water and drizzle over the vegetables, then sprinkle with thyme to serve.

Rosemary Olive-oil Over Shrooms N Asparagus

Servings: 6

Cooking Time: 15 Minutes

Ingredients:

- ½ pound fresh mushroom, quartered
- 1 bunch fresh asparagus, trimmed and cleaned
- 2 sprigs of fresh rosemary, minced
- 2 teaspoon olive oil
- salt and pepper to taste

Directions:

1. Preheat the air fryer to 400F.
2. Place the asparagus and mushrooms in a bowl and pour the rest of the ingredients.
3. Toss to coat the asparagus and mushrooms.
4. Place inside the air fryer and cook for 15 minutes.

Salted Garlic Zucchini Fries

Servings: 6

Cooking Time: 15 Minutes

Ingredients:

- ¼ teaspoon garlic powder
- ½ cup almond flour
- 2 large egg whites, beaten
- 3 medium zucchinis, sliced into fry sticks
- Salt and pepper to taste

Directions:

1. Preheat the air fryer for 5 minutes.
2. Mix all ingredients in a bowl until the zucchini fries are well coated.
3. Place in the air fryer basket.
4. Close and cook for 15 minutes for 425F.

Vegetable Tortilla Pizza

Servings: 1

Cooking Time: 15 Minutes

Ingredients:

- ¼ cup grated cheddar cheese
- ¼ cup grated mozzarella cheese
- 1 tbsp cooked sweet corn
- 4 zucchini slices
- 4 eggplant slices
- 4 red onion rings
- ½ green bell pepper, chopped
- 3 cherry tomatoes, quartered
- 1 tortilla
- ¼ tsp basil
- ¼ tsp oregano

Directions:

1. Preheat the air fryer to 350 F. Spread the tomato paste on the tortilla. Arrange the zucchini and eggplant slices first, then green peppers, and onion rings.
2. Arrange the cherry tomatoes and sprinkle the sweet corn over. Sprinkle with oregano and basil and

top with cheddar and mozzarella. Place in the fryer and cook for 10 minutes.

Cheesy Vegetable Quesadilla

Servings: 1
Cooking Time: 15 Minutes
Ingredients:
- ¼ cup shredded gouda cheese
- ¼ yellow bell pepper, sliced
- ¼ zucchini, sliced
- ½ green onion, sliced
- 1 tbsp cilantro, chopped
- 1 tsp olive oil

Directions:
1. Preheat the Air fryer to 390 F. Grease the air fryer basket with cooking spray.
2. Place a flour tortilla in the air fryer basket and top with gouda cheese, bell pepper, zucchini, cilantro, and green onion. Cover with the other tortilla and brush with olive oil. Cook for 10 minutes until lightly browned. When ready, cut into 4 wedges to serve.

Sesame Seeds Bok Choy(2)

Servings: 4
Cooking Time: 6 Minutes
Ingredients:
- 4 bunches spinach leaves
- 2 teaspoons sesame seeds
- 1 teaspoon garlic powder
- 1 teaspoon ginger powder
- Salt, to taste

Directions:
1. Preheat the Air fryer to 325F and grease an Air fryer basket.
2. Arrange the spinach leaves into the Air fryer basket and season with salt, garlic powder and ginger powder.
3. Cook for about 6 minutes, shaking once in between and dish out onto serving plates.
4. Top with sesame seeds and serve hot.

Cheesy Broccoli With Eggs

Servings: 4
Cooking Time: 15 Minutes
Ingredients:
- 4 eggs
- 1 cup cheese, shredded
- 1 cup cream
- 1 pinch nutmeg
- 1 tsp ginger powder
- salt and pepper to taste

Directions:
1. Steam the broccoli for 5 minutes. Then drain them and add 1 egg, cream, nutmeg, ginger, salt and pepper. Butter small ramekins and spread the mixture. Sprinkle the shredded cheese on top. Cook for 10 minutes at 280 F.

Roasted Mushrooms In Herb-garlic Oil

Servings: 4
Cooking Time: 25 Minutes
Ingredients:
- ½ teaspoon minced garlic
- 2 pounds mushrooms
- 2 teaspoons herbs de Provence
- 3 tablespoons coconut oil
- Salt and pepper to taste

Directions:
1. Preheat the air fryer for 5 minutes.
2. Place all ingredients in a baking dish that will fit in the air fryer.
3. Mix to combine.
4. Place the baking dish in the air fryer.
5. Cook for 25 minutes at 350F.

Nutty Pumpkin With Blue Cheese

Servings: 1
Cooking Time: 30 Minutes
Ingredients:

- 2 oz blue cheese, cubed
- 2 tbsp pine nuts
- 1 tbsp olive oil
- ½ cup baby spinach, packed
- 1 spring onion, sliced
- 1 radish, thinly sliced
- 1 tsp vinegar

Directions:

1. Preheat the air fryer to 330 F, and place the pine nuts in a baking dish to toast them for 5 minutes; set aside. Peel the pumpkin and chop it into small pieces. Place in the baking dish and toss with the olive oil. Increase the temperature to 390 F and cook the pumpkin for 20 minutes.

2. Place the pumpkin in a serving bowl. Add baby spinach, radish and spring onion; toss with the vinegar. Stir in the cubed blue cheese and top with the toasted pine nuts, to serve.

Classic Onion Rings

Servings: 8
Cooking Time: 30 Minutes

Ingredients:

- 2 medium-sized yellow onions, cut into rings
- 1 cup almond flour
- 1/2 teaspoon baking soda
- 1 teaspoon baking powder
- 1 ½ teaspoons sea salt flakes
- 2 medium-sized eggs
- 1 ½ cups plain milk
- 1 ¼ cups grated parmesan cheese
- 1/2 teaspoon green peppercorns, freshly cracked
- 1/2 teaspoon dried dill weed
- 1/4 teaspoon paprika

Directions:

1. Begin by preheating your Air Fryer to 356 degrees F.

2. Place the onion rings into the bowl with icy cold water; let them stay 15 to 20 minutes; drain the onion rings and dry them using a kitchen towel.

3. In a shallow bowl, mix the flour together with baking soda, baking powder and sea salt flakes. Then, coat each onion ring with the flour mixture;

4. In another shallow bowl, beat the eggs with milk; add the mixture to the remaining flour mixture and whisk well. Dredge the coated onion rings into this batter.

5. In a third bowl, mix the parmesan cheese, green peppercorns, dill, and paprika. Roll the onion rings over the parmesan cheese mixture, covering well.

6. Air-fry them in the cooking basket for 8 to 11 minutes or until thoroughly cooked to golden.

Warm Farro Salad With Roasted Tomatoes

Servings: 2
Cooking Time: 40 Minutes

Ingredients:

- 3/4 cup farro
- 3 cups water
- 1 tablespoon sea salt
- 1 pound cherry tomatoes
- 2 spring onions, chopped
- 2 carrots, grated
- 2 heaping tablespoons fresh parsley leaves
- 2 tablespoons champagne vinegar
- 2 tablespoons white wine
- 2 tablespoons extra-virgin olive oil
- 1 teaspoon red pepper flakes

Directions:

1. Place the farro, water, and salt in a saucepan and bring it to a rapid boil. Turn the heat down to medium-low, and simmer, covered, for 30 minutes or until the farro has softened.

2. Drain well and transfer to an air fryer-safe pan.

3. Meanwhile, place the cherry tomatoes in the lightly greased Air Fryer basket. Roast at 400 degrees F for 4 minutes.

4. Add the roasted tomatoes to the pan with the cooked farro, Toss the salad ingredients with the spring onions, carrots, parsley, vinegar, white wine, and olive oil.

5. Bake at 360 degrees F an additional 5 minutes. Serve garnished with red pepper flakes and enjoy!

Herby Veggie Cornish Pasties

Servings: 4
Cooking Time: 30 Minutes
Ingredients:

- ¼ cup mushrooms, chopped
- ¾ cup cold coconut oil
- 1 ½ cups plain flour
- 1 medium carrot, chopped
- 1 medium potato, diced
- 1 onion, sliced
- 1 stick celery, chopped
- 1 tablespoon nutritional yeast
- 1 tablespoon olive oil
- 1 teaspoon oregano
- a pinch of salt
- cold water for mixing the dough
- salt and pepper to taste

Directions:

1. Preheat the air fryer to 400F.
2. Prepare the dough by mixing the flour, coconut oil, and salt in a bowl. Use a fork and press the flour to combine everything. Gradually add a drop of water to the dough until you achieve a stiff consistency of the dough. Cover the dough with a cling film and let it rest for 30 minutes inside the fridge.
3. Roll the dough out and cut into squares. Set aside.
4. Heat olive oil over medium heat and sauté the onions for 2 minutes. Add the celery, carrots and potatoes. Continue stirring for 3 to 5 minutes before adding the mushrooms and oregano.
5. Season with salt and pepper to taste. Add nutritional yeast last. Let it cool and set aside.
6. Drop a tablespoon of vegetable mixture on to the dough and seal the edges of the dough with water.
7. Place inside the air fryer basket and cook for 20 minutes or until the dough is crispy.

Grilled 'n Spiced Tomatoes On Garden Salad

Servings: 4
Cooking Time: 20 Minutes
Ingredients:

- ¼ cup golden raisings
- ¼ cup hazelnuts, toasted and chopped
- ¼ cup pistachios, toasted and chopped
- ½ cup chopped chives
- ¾ cup cilantro leaves, chopped
- ¾ cup fresh parsley, chopped
- 1 clove of garlic, minced
- 2 tablespoons white balsamic vinegar
- 3 large green tomatoes
- 4 leaves iceberg lettuce
- 5 tablespoons olive oil
- Salt and pepper to taste

Directions:

1. Preheat the air fryer to 330F.
2. Place the grill pan accessory in the air fryer.
3. In a mixing bowl, season the tomatoes with garlic, oil, salt and pepper to taste.
4. Place on the grill pan and grill for 20 minutes.
5. Once the tomatoes are done, toss in a salad bowl together with the rest of the Ingredients.

Sweet & Spicy Parsnips

Servings: 6
Cooking Time: 44 Minutes
Ingredients:

- 2 pounds parsnip, peeled and cut into 1-inch chunks
- 1 tablespoon butter, melted
- 2 tablespoons honey
- 1 tablespoon dried parsley flakes, crushed
- ¼ teaspoon red pepper flakes, crushed
- Salt and ground black pepper, as required

Directions:

1. Set the temperature of air fryer to 355 degrees F. Grease an air fryer basket.

2. In a large bowl, mix together the parsnips and butter.

3. Arrange parsnip chunks into the prepared air fryer basket in a single layer.

4. Air fry for about 40 minutes.

5. Meanwhile, in another large bowl, mix well remaining ingredients.

6. After 40 minutes, transfer parsnips into the bowl of honey mixture and toss to coat well.

7. Again, arrange the parsnip chunks into air fryer basket in a single layer.

8. Air fry for 3-4 more minutes.

9. Remove from air fryer and transfer the parsnip chunks onto serving plates.

10. Serve hot.

Curried Cauliflower Florets

Servings: 4

Cooking Time: 34 Minutes

Ingredients:

- Salt to taste
- 1 ½ tbsp curry powder
- ½ cup olive oil
- ⅓ cup fried pine nuts

Directions:

1. Preheat the air fryer to 390 F, and mix the pine nuts and 1 tsp of olive oil, in a medium bowl. Pour them in the air fryer's basket and cook for 2 minutes; remove to cool.

2. Place the cauliflower on a cutting board. Use a knife to cut them into 1-inch florets. Place them in a large mixing bowl. Add the curry powder, salt, and the remaining olive oil; mix well. Place the cauliflower florets in the fryer's basket in 2 batches, and cook each batch for 10 minutes. Remove the curried florets onto a serving platter, sprinkle with the pine nuts, and toss. Serve the florets with tomato sauce or as a side to a meat dish.

Indian Aloo Tikka

Servings: 2

Cooking Time: 20 Minutes

Ingredients:

- 3 tbsp lemon juice
- 1 bell pepper, sliced
- Salt and pepper to taste
- 2 onions, chopped
- 4 tbsp fennel
- 5 tbsp flour
- 2 tbsp ginger-garlic paste
- ½ cup mint leaves, chopped
- 2 cups cilantro, chopped

Directions:

1. Preheat your air fryer to 360 F.

2. In a bowl, mix cilantro, mint, fennel, ginger garlic paste, flour, salt and lemon juice. Blend to form a paste and add potato. In another bowl, mix bell pepper, onions and fennel mixture. Blend the mixture until you have a thick mix. Divide the mixture evenly into 5-6 cakes. Add the prepared potato cakes into your air fryer and cook for 15 minutes. Serve with ketchup.

Low-calorie Beets Dish

Servings: 2

Cooking Time: 20 Minutes

Ingredients:

- ⅓ cup balsamic vinegar
- 1 tbsp olive oil
- 1 tbsp honey
- Salt and pepper to taste
- 2 springs rosemary

Directions:

1. In a bowl, mix rosemary, pepper, salt, vinegar and honey. Cover beets with the prepared sauce and then coat with oil. Preheat your air fryer to 400 F, and cook the beets in the air fryer for 10 minutes. Pour the balsamic vinegar in a pan over medium heat; bring to a boil and cook until reduced by half. Drizzle the beets with balsamic glaze, to serve.

Garden Fresh Green Beans

Servings: 4

Cooking Time: 12 Minutes

Ingredients:

- 1 pound green beans, washed and trimmed
- 1 teaspoon butter, melted
- 1 tablespoon fresh lemon juice
- ¼ teaspoon garlic powder
- Salt and freshly ground pepper, to taste

Directions:

1. Preheat the Air fryer to 400F and grease an Air fryer basket.
2. Put all the ingredients in a large bowl and transfer into the Air fryer basket.
3. Cook for about 8 minutes and dish out in a bowl to serve warm.

Sweet & Spicy Cauliflower

Servings: 4

Cooking Time: 30 Minutes

Ingredients:

- 1 head cauliflower, cut into florets
- ¾ cup onion, thinly sliced
- 5 garlic cloves, finely sliced
- 1½ tablespoons soy sauce
- 1 tablespoon hot sauce
- 1 tablespoon rice vinegar
- 1 teaspoon coconut sugar
- Pinch of red pepper flakes
- Ground black pepper, as required
- 2 scallions, chopped

Directions:

1. Set the temperature of air fryer to 350 degrees F. Grease an air fryer pan.
2. Arrange cauliflower florets into the prepared air fryer pan in a single layer.
3. Air fry for about 10 minutes.
4. Remove from air fryer and stir in the onions.
5. Air fry for another 10 minutes.
6. Remove from air fryer and stir in the garlic.
7. Air fry for 5 more minutes.

8. Meanwhile, in a bowl, mix well soy sauce, hot sauce, vinegar, coconut sugar, red pepper flakes, and black pepper.
9. Remove from the air fryer and stir in the sauce mixture.
10. Air fry for about 5 minutes.
11. Remove from air fryer and transfer the cauliflower mixture onto serving plates.
12. Garnish with scallions and serve.

Prawn Toast

Servings: 2

Cooking Time: 12 Minutes

Ingredients:

- 1 large spring onion, finely sliced
- 3 white bread slices
- ½ cup sweet corn
- 1 egg white, whisked
- 1 tbsp black sesame seeds

Directions:

1. In a bowl, place prawns, corn, spring onion and the sesame seeds. Add the whisked egg and mix the ingredients. Spread the mixture over the bread slices. Place in the prawns in the air fryer's basket and sprinkle oil. Fry the prawns until golden, for 8-10 minutes at 370 F. Serve with ketchup or chili sauce.

Sautéed Bacon With Spinach

Servings: 2

Cooking Time: 9 Minutes

Ingredients:

- 3 meatless bacon slices, chopped
- 1 onion, chopped
- 4-ounce fresh spinach
- 2 tablespoons olive oil
- 1 garlic clove, minced

Directions:

1. Preheat the Air fryer to 340F and grease an Air fryer pan.
2. Put olive oil and garlic in the Air fryer pan and place in the Air fryer basket.

3. Cook for about 2 minutes and add bacon and onions.
4. Cook for about 3 minutes and stir in the spinach.
5. Cook for about 4 minutes and dish out in a bowl to serve.

Sautéed Green Beans

Servings: 2
Cooking Time: 10 Minutes
Ingredients:
- 8 ounces fresh green beans, trimmed and cut in half
- 1 teaspoon sesame oil
- 1 tablespoon soy sauce

Directions:
1. Preheat the Air fryer to 390F and grease an Air fryer basket.
2. Mix green beans, soy sauce, and sesame oil in a bowl and toss to coat well.
3. Arrange green beans into the Air fryer basket and cook for about 10 minutes, tossing once in between.
4. Dish out onto serving plates and serve hot.

Veggie Skewers

Servings: 4
Cooking Time: 20 Minutes
Ingredients:
- 1 cup canned beans
- ⅓ cup grated carrots
- 2 boiled and mashed potatoes
- ¼ cup chopped fresh mint leaves
- ½ tsp garam masala powder
- ½ cup paneer
- 1 green chili
- 1-inch piece of fresh ginger
- 3 garlic cloves
- Salt, to taste

Directions:

1. Soak 12 skewers until ready to use. Preheat the air fryer to 390 F, and place the beans, carrots, garlic, ginger, chili, paneer, and mint, in a food processor; process until smooth, then transfer to a bowl.
2. Add the mashed potatoes, cornflour, some salt, and garam masala powder to the bowl; mix until fully incorporated. Divide the mixture into 12 equal pieces. Shape each of the pieces around a skewer. Cook skewers for 10 minutes.

Tender Butternut Squash Fry

Servings: 2
Cooking Time: 10 Minutes
Ingredients:
- 1 tablespoon cooking oil
- 1-pound butternut squash, seeded and sliced
- Salt and pepper to taste

Directions:
1. Place the grill pan accessory in the air fryer.
2. In a bowl, place all Ingredients and toss to coat and season the squash.
3. Place in the grill pan.
4. Close the air fryer and cook for 10 minutes at 330F.

Cottage And Mayonnaise Stuffed Peppers

Servings: 2
Cooking Time: 20 Minutes
Ingredients:
- 1 red bell pepper, top and seeds removed
- 1 yellow bell pepper, top and seeds removed
- Salt and pepper, to taste
- 1 cup Cottage cheese
- 4 tablespoons mayonnaise
- 2 pickles, chopped

Directions:
1. Arrange the peppers in the lightly greased cooking basket. Cook in the preheated Air Fryer at 400 degrees F for 15 minutes, turning them over halfway through the cooking time.
2. Season with salt and pepper.

3. Then, in a mixing bowl, combine the cream cheese with the mayonnaise and chopped pickles. Stuff the pepper with the cream cheese mixture and serve. Enjoy!

Teriyaki Cauliflower4

Servings: 4
Cooking Time: 20 Minutes
Ingredients:
- ½ cup soy sauce
- 3 tbsp brown sugar
- 1 tsp sesame oil
- ⅓ cup water
- ½ chili powder
- 2 cloves garlic, chopped
- 1 tsp cornstarch

Directions:
1. In a bowl, whisk soy sauce, sugar, sesame oil, water, chili powder, garlic and cornstarch, until smooth. In a bowl, add cauliflower, and pour teriyaki sauce over the top, toss with hands until well-coated.
2. Take the cauliflower to the air fryer's basket and cook for 14 minutes at 340 F, turning once halfway through. When ready, check if the cauliflower is cooked but not too soft. Serve with rice.

Quinoa Bowl With Lime-sriracha

Servings: 4
Cooking Time: 10 Minutes
Ingredients:
- ¼ cup soy sauce
- 1 block extra firm tofu
- 1 red bell pepper, sliced
- 1 tablespoon sriracha
- 1-pound fresh broccoli florets, blanched
- 2 cups quinoa, cooked according to package instruction
- 2 tablespoons lime juice
- 2 tablespoons sesame oil
- 3 medium carrots, peeled and thinly sliced

- 3 tablespoons molasses
- 8 ounces spinach, blanched
- Salt and pepper to taste

Directions:
1. Season tofu with sesame oil, salt and pepper.
2. Place the grill pan accessory in the air fryer.
3. Place the seasoned tofu on the grill pan accessory.
4. Close the air fryer and cook for 10 minutes at 330F.
5. Stir the tofu to brown all sides evenly.
6. Set aside and arrange the Buddha bowl.
7. In a mixing bowl, combine the soy sauce, molasses, lime juice and sriracha. Set aside.
8. Place quinoa in bowls and top with broccoli, carrots, red bell pepper, and spinach.
9. Top in tofu and drizzle with the sauce last.

Quinoa & Veggie Stuffed Peppers

Servings: 1
Cooking Time: 16 Minutes
Ingredients:
- 1 bell pepper
- ½ tbsp diced onion
- ½ diced tomato, plus one tomato slice
- ¼ tsp smoked paprika
- Salt and pepper, to taste
- 1 tsp olive oil
- ¼ tsp dried basil

Directions:
1. Preheat the air fryer to 350 F, core and clean the bell pepper to prepare it for stuffing. Brush the pepper with half of the olive oil on the outside. In a small bowl, combine all of the other ingredients, except the tomato slice and reserved half-teaspoon of olive oil.
2. Stuff the pepper with the filling and top with the tomato slice. Brush the tomato slice with the remaining half-teaspoon of olive oil and sprinkle with basil. Air fry for 10 minutes, until thoroughly cooked.

Mashed Potatoes With Roasted Peppers

Servings: 4
Cooking Time: 1 Hour
Ingredients:

- 4 potatoes
- 1 tablespoon vegan margarine
- 1 teaspoon garlic powder
- 1 pound bell peppers, seeded and quartered lengthwise
- 2 Fresno peppers, seeded and halved lengthwise
- 4 tablespoons olive oil
- 2 tablespoons cider vinegar
- 4 garlic cloves, pressed
- Kosher salt, to taste
- 1/2 teaspoon freshly ground black pepper
- 1/2 teaspoon dried dill

Directions:

1.   Place the potatoes in the Air Fryer basket and cook at 400 degrees F for 40 minutes. Discard the skin and mash the potatoes with the vegan margarine and garlic powder.
2.   Then, roast the peppers at 400 degrees F for 5 minutes. Give the peppers a half turn; place them back in the cooking basket and roast for another 5 minutes.
3.   Turn them one more time and roast until the skin is charred and soft or 5 more minutes. Peel the peppers and let them cool to room temperature.
4.   Toss your peppers with the remaining ingredients and serve with the mashed potatoes. Bon appétit!

Cheesy Green Beans With Mushrooms And Peppers

Servings: 3
Cooking Time: 15 Minutes
Ingredients:

- 1 tablespoon extra-virgin olive oil
- 2 garlic cloves, minced
- 1/2 cup scallions, chopped
- 2 cups oyster mushrooms, sliced

- 2 Italian peppers, deseeded and sliced
- 1/2 pound green beans, trimmed
- 1/2 teaspoon mustard seeds
- Sea salt and ground black pepper, to taste
- 1 cup cream cheese

Directions:

1.   Start by preheating your Air Fryer to 390 degrees F. Heat the oil and sauté the garlic and scallions until tender and fragrant, about 5 minutes.
2.   Add the remaining ingredients and stir to combine well.
3.   Increase the temperature to 400 degrees F and cook for a further 5 minutes. Serve warm.

Roasted Brussels Sprouts & Pine Nuts

Servings: 6
Cooking Time: 20 Minutes
Ingredients:

- 1 tbsp olive oil
- 1 ¾ oz raisins, soaked
- Juice of 1 orange
- salt to taste
- 1 ¾ oz toasted pine nuts

Directions:

1.   Preheat your air fryer to 392 F. In a bowl, pop the sprouts with oil and salt and stir to combine well. Add the sprouts to the air fryer and roast for 15 minutes. Mix with toasted pine nuts and soaked raisins. Drizzle with orange juice to serve.

Cheesy Stuffed Peppers

Servings: 4
Cooking Time: 40 Minutes
Ingredients:

- Salt and pepper to taste
- ½ cup olive oil
- 1 red onion, chopped
- 1 large tomato, chopped
- ½ cup crumbled Goat cheese
- 3 cups cauliflower, chopped

- 2 tbsp grated Parmesan cheese
- 2 tbsp chopped basil
- 1 tbsp lemon zest

Directions:

1. Preheat the air fryer to 350 F, and cut the peppers a quarter way from the head down and lengthwise. Remove the membrane and seeds. Season the peppers with pepper, salt, and drizzle olive oil over. Place the pepper bottoms in the fryer's basket and cook for 5 minutes at 350 F to soften a little bit.

2. In a mixing bowl, add tomatoes, goat cheese, lemon zest, basil, and cauliflower and season with salt and pepper; mix well. Remove the bottoms from the air fryer to a flat surface and spoon the cheese mixture into them. Sprinkle with Parmesan cheese and return to the basket; cook for 15 minutes.

Veggie Wontons With Chili-oil Seasoning

Servings: 4

Cooking Time: 10 Minutes

Ingredients:

- ½ cup chopped mushrooms
- ½ cup grated carrots
- ½ cup grated white onion
- ½ teaspoon white pepper
- ¾ cup chopped red pepper
- ¾ cup grated cabbage
- 1 tablespoon chili sauce
- 1 teaspoon garlic powder
- 2 tablespoons olive oil
- 30 wonton wrappers
- Salt to taste
- Water for sealing wontons

Directions:

1. In a skillet over medium heat, place all vegetables and cook until all moisture have been released from the vegetables.

2. Remove from the heat and season with chili sauce, garlic powder, white pepper, and salt.

3. Put wanton wrapper on a working surface and add a tablespoon of the vegetable mixture in the middle of the wrapper. Wet the edges of the wonton wrapper with water and fold the wrapper to close.

4. Brush with oil and place in the double layer rack.

5. Place the rack with the wonton in the air fryer.

6. Close the air fryer and cook for 10 minutes at 330F.

Mom's Veggie Fritters

Servings: 3

Cooking Time: 30 Minutes

Ingredients:

- 1 cup celery, chopped
- 1 cup cauliflower rice
- 2 garlic cloves, minced
- 1 shallot, chopped
- Sea salt and ground black pepper, to taste
- 2 tablespoons fresh parsley, chopped
- 1 egg, well beaten
- 1 cup Romano cheese, grated
- 1/2 cup almond flour
- 1 tablespoon olive oil

Directions:

1. Mix the veggies, spices, egg, almond flour, and Romano cheese until everything is well incorporated.

2. Take 1 tablespoon of the veggie mixture and roll into a ball. Roll the balls onto the dried bread flakes. Brush the veggie balls with olive oil on all sides.

3. Cook in the preheated Air Fryer at 360 degrees F for 15 minutes or until thoroughly cooked and crispy.

4. Repeat the process until you run out of ingredients. Bon appétit!

Open-faced Vegan Flatbread-wich

Servings: 4

Cooking Time: 25 Minutes

Ingredients:

- 1 can chickpeas, drained and rinsed
- 1 medium-sized head of cauliflower, cut into florets
- 1 tablespoon extra-virgin olive oil

- 2 ripe avocados, mashed
- 2 tablespoons lemon juice
- 4 flatbreads, toasted
- salt and pepper to taste

Directions:

1. Preheat the air fryer to 425F.
2. In a mixing bowl, combine the cauliflower, chickpeas, olive oil, and lemon juice. Season with salt and pepper to taste.
3. Place inside the air fryer basket and cook for 25 minutes.
4. Once cooked, place on half of the flatbread and add avocado mash.
5. Season with more salt and pepper to taste.
6. Serve with hot sauce.

Mushroom Loaf

Servings: 2
Cooking Time: 20 Minutes

Ingredients:

- 2 cups mushrooms, chopped
- ½ cups cheddar cheese, shredded
- ¾ cup flour
- 2 tbsp. butter, melted
- 2 eggs

Directions:

1. In a food processor, pulse together the mushrooms, cheese, flour, melted butter, and eggs, along with some salt and pepper if desired, until a uniform consistency is achieved.
2. Transfer into a silicone loaf pan, spreading and levelling with a palette knife.
3. Pre-heat the fryer at 375°F and put the rack inside.
4. Set the loaf pan on the rack and cook for fifteen minutes.
5. Take care when removing the pan from the fryer and leave it to cool. Then slice and serve.

Mushroom 'n Bell Pepper Pizza

Servings: 10

Cooking Time: 10 Minutes

Ingredients:

- ¼ red bell pepper, chopped
- 1 cup oyster mushrooms, chopped
- 1 shallot, chopped
- 1 vegan pizza dough
- 2 tablespoons parsley
- salt and pepper

Directions:

1. Preheat the air fryer to 400F.
2. Slice the pizza dough into squares. Set aside.
3. In a mixing bowl, mix together the oyster mushroom, shallot, bell pepper and parsley.
4. Season with salt and pepper to taste.
5. Place the topping on top of the pizza squares.
6. Place inside the air fryer and cook for 10 minutes.

Stuffed Eggplant

Servings: 2
Cooking Time: 35 Minutes

Ingredients:

- large eggplant
- ¼ medium yellow onion, diced
- 2 tbsp. red bell pepper, diced
- 1 cup spinach
- ¼ cup artichoke hearts, chopped

Directions:

1. Cut the eggplant lengthwise into slices and spoon out the flesh, leaving a shell about a half-inch thick. Chop it up and set aside.
2. Set a skillet over a medium heat and spritz with cooking spray. Cook the onions for about three to five minutes to soften. Then add the pepper, spinach, artichokes, and the flesh of eggplant. Fry for a further five minutes, then remove from the heat.
3. Scoop this mixture in equal parts into the eggplant shells and place each one in the fryer.
4. Cook for twenty minutes at 320°F until the eggplant shells are soft. Serve warm.

Fried Spicy Tofu

Servings: 4
Cooking Time: 55 Minutes
Ingredients:

- 16 ounces firm tofu, pressed and cubed
- 1 tablespoon vegan oyster sauce
- 1 tablespoon tamari sauce
- 1 teaspoon cider vinegar
- 1 teaspoon pure maple syrup
- 1 teaspoon sriracha
- 1/2 teaspoon shallot powder
- 1/2 teaspoon porcini powder
- 1 teaspoon garlic powder
- 1 tablespoon sesame oil
- 2 tablespoons golden flaxseed meal

Directions:

1. Toss the tofu with the oyster sauce, tamari sauce, vinegar, maple syrup, sriracha, shallot powder, porcini powder, garlic powder, and sesame oil. Let it marinate for 30 minutes.
2. Toss the marinated tofu with the flaxseed meal.
3. Cook at 360 degrees F for 10 minutes; turn them over and cook for 12 minutes more. Bon appétit!

Almond-apple Treat

Servings: 4
Cooking Time: 15 Minutes
Ingredients:

- 1 ½ oz almonds
- ¾ oz raisins
- 2 tbsp sugar

Directions:

1. Preheat air fryer to 360 F. In a bowl, mix sugar, almonds, and raisins. Blend the mixture with a hand mixer. Fill apples with almond mixture. Place in air fryer's basket and cook for 10 minutes. Serve.

Mozzarella Cabbage With Blue Cheese

Servings: 4
Cooking Time: 25 Minutes
Ingredients:

- 2 cups Parmesan cheese, chopped
- 4 tbsp melted butter
- Salt and pepper to taste
- ½ cup blue cheese sauce

Directions:

1. Preheat your air fryer to 380 F, and cover cabbage wedges with melted butter; coat with mozzarella. Place the coated cabbage in the cooking basket and cook for 20 minutes. Serve with blue cheese.

Curry 'n Coriander Spiced Bread Rolls

Servings: 5
Cooking Time: 15 Minutes
Ingredients:

- ½ teaspoon mustard seeds
- ½ teaspoon turmeric
- 1 bunch coriander, chopped
- 1 tablespoon olive oil
- 2 green chilies, seeded and chopped
- 2 small onions, chopped
- 2 sprigs, curry leaves
- 5 large potatoes, boiled
- 8 slices of vegan wheat bread, brown sides discarded
- salt and pepper to taste

Directions:

1. In a bowl, mash the potatoes and season with salt and pepper to taste. Set aside.
2. Heat olive oil in a skillet over medium low flame and add the mustard seeds. Stir until the seeds sputter. Then add the onions and fry until translucent. Stir in the turmeric powder and curry leaves. Continue to cook for 2 more minutes until fragrant. Remove from heat and add to the potatoes. Stir in the green chilies and coriander. This will be the filling.
3. Wet the bread and remove the excess water.
4. Place a tablespoon of the potato mixture in the middle of the bread and gently roll the bread in so

that the potato filling is completely sealed inside the bread.

5. Brush with oil and place inside the air fryer.

6. Cook in a 400F preheated air fryer for 15 minutes. Make sure to shake the air fryer basket gently halfway through the cooking time for even cooking.

Easy Vegan "chicken"

Servings: 4

Cooking Time: 20 Minutes

Ingredients:

- 8 ounces soy chunks
- 1/2 cup cornmeal
- 1/4 cup all-purpose flour
- 1 teaspoon cayenne pepper
- 1/2 teaspoon mustard powder
- 1 teaspoon celery seeds
- Sea salt and ground black pepper, to taste

Directions:

1. Boil the soya chunks in lots of water in a saucepan over medium-high heat. Remove from the heat and let them soak for 10 minutes.

2. Drain, rinse, and squeeze off the excess water.

3. Mix the remaining ingredients in a bowl. Roll the soy chunks over the breading mixture, pressing to adhere.

4. Arrange the soy chunks in the lightly greased Air Fryer basket.

5. Cook in the preheated Air Fryer at 390 degrees for 10 minutes, turning them over halfway through the cooking time; work in batches. Bon appétit!

Cauliflower Steak With Thick Sauce

Servings: 2

Cooking Time: 15 Minutes

Ingredients:

- ¼ cup almond milk
- ¼ teaspoon vegetable stock powder
- 1 cauliflower, sliced into two
- 1 tablespoon olive oil

- 2 tablespoons onion, chopped
- salt and pepper to taste

Directions:

1. Soak the cauliflower in salted water or brine for at least 2 hours.

2. Preheat the air fryer to 400F.

3. Rinse the cauliflower and place inside the air fryer and cook for 15 minutes.

4. Meanwhile, heat oil in a skillet over medium flame. Sauté the onions and stir until translucent. Add the vegetable stock powder and milk.

5. Bring to boil and adjust the heat to low.

6. Allow the sauce to reduce and season with salt and pepper.

7. Place cauliflower steak on a plate and pour over sauce.

Cheesy Spinach

Servings: 3

Cooking Time: 15 Minutes

Ingredients:

- 1 (10-ounces) package frozen spinach, thawed
- ½ cup onion, chopped
- 2 teaspoons garlic, minced
- 4 ounces cream cheese, chopped
- ½ teaspoon ground nutmeg
- Salt and ground black pepper, as required
- ¼ cup Parmesan cheese, shredded

Directions:

1. In a bowl, mix well spinach, onion, garlic, cream cheese, nutmeg, salt, and black pepper.

2. Set the temperature of air fryer to 350 degrees F. Grease an air fryer pan.

3. Place spinach mixture into the prepared air fryer pan.

4. Air fry for about 10 minutes.

5. Remove from air fryer and stir the mixture well.

6. Sprinkle the spinach mixture evenly with Parmesan cheese.

7. Now, set the temperature of air fryer to 400 degrees F and air fry for 5 more minutes.

8. Remove from air fryer and transfer the spinach mixture onto serving plates.

9. Serve hot.

Spaghetti Squash

Servings: 2

Cooking Time: 45 Minutes

Ingredients:

- spaghetti squash
- 1 tsp. olive oil
- Salt and pepper
- 4 tbsp. heavy cream
- 1 tsp. butter

Directions:

1. Pre-heat your fryer at 360°F.

2. Cut and de-seed the spaghetti squash. Brush with the olive oil and season with salt and pepper to taste.

3. Put the squash inside the fryer, placing it cut-side-down. Cook for thirty minutes. Halfway through cooking, fluff the spaghetti inside the squash with a fork.

4. When the squash is ready, fluff the spaghetti some more, then pour some heavy cream and butter over it and give it a good stir. Serve with the low-carb tomato sauce of your choice.

Paneer Cutlet

Servings: 1

Cooking Time: 15 Minutes

Ingredients:

- 1 cup grated cheese
- ½ tsp chai masala
- 1 tsp butter
- ½ tsp garlic powder
- 1 small onion, finely chopped
- ½ tsp oregano
- ½ tsp salt

Directions:

1. Preheat the air fryer to 350 F, and grease a baking dish. Mix all ingredients in a bowl, until well

incorporated. Make cutlets out of the mixture and place them on the greased baking dish. Place the baking dish in the air fryer and cook the cutlets for 10 minutes, until crispy.

Aromatic Baked Potatoes With Chives

Servings: 2

Cooking Time: 45 Minutes

Ingredients:

- 4 medium baking potatoes, peeled
- 2 tablespoons olive oil
- 1/4 teaspoon red pepper flakes
- 1/4 teaspoon smoked paprika
- 1 tablespoon sea salt
- 2 garlic cloves, minced
- 2 tablespoons chives, chopped

Directions:

1. Toss the potatoes with the olive oil, seasoning, and garlic.

2. Place them in the Air Fryer basket. Cook in the preheated Air Fryer at 400 degrees F for 40 minutes or until fork tender.

3. Garnish with fresh chopped chives. Bon appétit!

Kurkuri Bhindi (indian Fried Okra)

Servings: 4

Cooking Time: 20 Minutes

Ingredients:

- 2 tbsp garam masala
- 1 cup cornmeal
- ¼ cup flour
- Salt to taste
- ½ pound okra, trimmed and halved lengthwise
- 1 egg

Directions:

1. Preheat the Air Fryer to 380 F.

2. In a bowl, mix cornmeal, flour, chili powder, garam masala, salt, and pepper. In another bowl, whisk the egg; season with salt and pepper. Dip the okra in the egg and then coat in cornmeal mixture.

Spray okra with cooking spray and place in the air fryer basket in a single layer. Cook for 6 minutes. Slide out the basket and shake; cook for another 6 minutes until golden brown. Serve with your favorite dip.

Veggie Rice

Servings: 2
Cooking Time: 18 Minutes
Ingredients:
- 2 cups cooked white rice
- 1 large egg, lightly beaten
- ½ cup frozen peas, thawed
- ½ cup frozen carrots, thawed
- ½ teaspoon sesame seeds, toasted
- 1 tablespoon vegetable oil
- 2 teaspoons sesame oil, toasted and divided
- 1 tablespoon water
- Salt and ground white pepper, as required
- 1 teaspoon soy sauce
- 1 teaspoon Sriracha sauce

Directions:
1. Preheat the Air fryer to 380F and grease an Air fryer pan.
2. Mix the rice, vegetable oil, 1 teaspoon of sesame oil, water, salt, and white pepper in a bowl.
3. Transfer the rice mixture into the Air fryer basket and cook for about 12 minutes.
4. Pour the beaten egg over rice and cook for about 4 minutes.
5. Stir in the peas and carrots and cook for 2 more minutes.
6. Meanwhile, mix soy sauce, Sriracha sauce, sesame seeds and the remaining sesame oil in a bowl.
7. Dish out the potato cubes onto serving plates and drizzle with sauce to serve.

Tofu With Orange Sauce

Servings: 4
Cooking Time: 20 Minutes
Ingredients:
- 1 pound extra-firm tofu, pressed and cubed
- ½ cup water
- 4 teaspoons cornstarch, divided
- 2 scallions (green part), chopped
- 1 tablespoon tamari
- 1/3 cup fresh orange juice
- 1 tablespoon honey
- 1 teaspoon orange zest, grated
- 1 teaspoon garlic, minced
- 1 teaspoon fresh ginger, minced
- ¼ teaspoon red pepper flakes, crushed

Directions:
1. Preheat the Air fryer to 390F and grease an Air fryer basket.
2. Mix the tofu, cornstarch, and tamari in a bowl and toss to coat well.
3. Arrange half of the tofu pieces in the Air fryer pan and cook for about 10 minutes.
4. Repeat with the remaining tofu and dish out in a bowl.
5. Put all the ingredients except scallions in a small pan over medium-high heat and bring to a boil.
6. Pour this sauce over the tofu and garnish with scallions to serve.

Brussels Sprouts With Garlic Aioli

Servings: 4
Cooking Time: 25 Minutes
Ingredients:
- Salt and pepper to taste
- 1 ½ tbsp olive oil
- 2 tsp lemon juice
- 1 tsp powdered chili
- 3 cloves garlic
- ¾ cup mayonnaise, whole egg
- 2 cups water

Directions:
1. Place a skillet over medium heat, add the garlic cloves with the peels on it and roast until lightly brown and fragrant. Remove the skillet and place a pot with water over the same heat; bring to a boil.

Add in Brussels sprouts and blanch for 3 minutes. Drain and set aside.

2. Preheat air fryer to 350 F. Remove the garlic from the skillet to a plate; peel, crush and set aside. Add olive oil to the skillet and light the fire to medium heat. Stir in the Brussels sprouts, season with pepper and salt; sauté for 2 minutes. Pour the brussels sprouts in the fryer's basket and cook for 5 minutes.

3. In a bowl, add mayonnaise, crushed garlic, lemon juice, powdered chili, pepper and salt; mix well. Remove the brussels sprouts onto a serving bowl and serve with the garlic aioli.

APPENDIX : RECIPES INDEX